I0837167

THE VISIGOTHIC MARK

This is a red-letter and interlinear Gospel of Mark in both the surviving Gothic and in English, for the faithful and for linguists. Not since Bosworth in 1888 has there existed such a printed, Biblical, English/Gothic interlinear text.

Ed. by Gregory Scaff

The Visigothic Mark.
Second Edition.
ISBN: 978-0-9970129-3-4

https://succubusmedia3.webnode.page/
https://gregoryscaff.webnode.page
Facebook: Succubus Arts—Gregory Scaff
YouTube: Succubus Media
https://www.youtube.com/watch?v=DXbs8Pb5rvU
Twitter: @gregoryscaff

Printed in the United States of America.

ACKNOWLEDGEMENTS

Much appreciation to James Byrne & to Professor Pagliarulo for their kind words.

Thanks to St. Wulfila.

Thanks to King James.

Many thanks and love to Robert and Rolande Scaff who gifted me a rare copy of Streitberg's Gotische Bibel. I could not have done this without you.

This book began as a personal project to aid in my studies. I hope you find this journey as useful and as inspiring as I have.

DEDICATION

Du Nyla, Diswissula, qenaÏ meinaÏ þÏzaÏ lÏuboston.

To the love of my life, the blindingly sparkly Muffin,

INTRODUCTION

The Gothic language has nothing to do with wombats, cantaloupe, or the group of black-wearing folks called goths today.

Gothic is an extinct East Germanic language, related to modern languages such as the West Germanic languages Old English or Frisian, and the North Germanic languages Icelandic or Danish.

A devout fourth century Goth named Wulfila dedicated his life to bringing Christianity to the Visigoths. Wulfila's converts became the first European church founded outside of the Roman Empire. Bishop Wulfila translated the Bible into Gothic; his translation was to be read for centuries to come.

Herein is the surviving text of Wulfila's translation of the Gospel of Mark.

The reader is urged to read the resources listed for further information.

TEXTUAL NOTES

Gaps in the surviving Gothic text are marked by ellipsis: . . .

Words in italics are added for clarification or are reasonably inferred to have been written originally.

Every effort has been made to bring you the most current and accurate Gothic text. I used the public domain KJV for the English, and the public domain Wright for the Gothic. The Gothic text is in Roman letters for the convenience of beginners.

The font Georgia size 10 was used for beauty and clarity.

All errors are mine.

AIWAGGELJO THAIRH MARKU.

Chapter I ANASTŌDEIÞ

1:1 Anastōdeíns
aíwaggēlyōns Iēsuis Xristáus
sunáus Gudis.
2 Swē gamēliþ ist in Esaïin
praúfetáu, sái, ik insandya
aggilu meinana faúra þus,
saei gamanweiþ wig þeinana
faúra þus.
3 Stibna wōpyandins in
áuþidái, manweiþ wig
fráuyins, raíhtōs waúrkeiþ
stáigōs Gudis unsaris.
4 Was Iōhannēs dáupyands
in áuþidái yah mēryands
dáupein idreigōs du
aflageinái frawaúrhtē.
5 Yah usiddyēdun du imma
all Iudaialand yah
laírusaúlwmeis, yah
dáupidái wēsun allái in
laúrdanē aƕái fram imma,
andháitandans frawaúrhtim
seináim.
6 Wasuþ-þan īōhannēs
gawasiþs taglam ulbandáus
yah gaírda filleina bi hup
seinana, yah matida
þramsteins yah miliþ
háiþiwisk,
7 yah mērida qiþand, qimiþ
swinþōza mis sa afar mis,
þizei ik ni im waírþs
anahneiwands andbindan
skáudaráip skōhē is.
8 Aþþan ik dáupya izwis in
watin, iþ is dáupeiþ izwis in
Ahmin Weihamma

THE GOSPEL ACCORDING TO MARK

Chapter 1 THE BEGINNING

1:1 The beginning of the
gospel of Jesus Christ, Son
of God;
2 As is written in the
prophets, Behold, I send my
messenger before thy face,
which shall prepare thy way
before thee.
3 The voice of one crying in
the wilderness, prepare ye
the way of the Lord, make
his paths straight.
4 John did baptize in the
wilderness, and preach the
baptism of repentance for
the remission of sins.
5 And there went out unto
him all the land of Judaea,
and they of Jerusalem, and
were all baptized of him in
the river of Jordan,
confessing their sins.
6 And John was clothed
with camel's hair and with a
girdle of skin about his
loins; and he did eat locusts
and wild honey;
7 And preached, saying,
there comes one mightier
than I after me, the latchet
of whose shoes I am not
worthy to stoop down and
unloose.
8 I indeed have baptized
you with water, but he shall
baptize you with the Holy
Ghost.

9 Yah warþ in yáináim
dagam, qam Iēsus fram
Nazaraíþ Galeilaias, yah
dáupiþs was fram Iōhannē
in Iaúrdanē.
10 Yah suns usgaggands us
þamma watin gasaƕ
uslukanans himinans, yah
ahman swē ahak
atgaggandan ana ina.
11 Yah stibna qam us
himinam, þu is sunus meins
sa liuba, in þuzei waíla
galeikáida.

12 Yah suns sái, ahma ina
ustáuh in áuþida.

13 Yah was in þizái áuþidái
dagē fidwōr tiguns fráisans
fram Satanin, yah was miþ
diuzam, yah aggileis
andbahtidēdun imma.
14 Iþ afar þatei atgibans
warþ Iōhannēs, qam Iēsus in
Gateilaia mēryands
aíwaggēlyōn þiudangardyōs
Gudis,
15 qiþands þatei usfullnōda
þata mēl yah atnēƕida sik
þiudangardi Gudis: idreigōþ
yah galáubeiþ in
aíwaggēlyōn.
16 Yah ƕarbōnds faúr
marein Galeilaias gasaƕ
Seimōnu yah Andraían
brōþar is, þis Seimō-nis,
waírpandans nati in marein,
wēsun auk fiskyans.
17 Yah qaþ im Iēsus: hiryats
afar mis, yah gatáuya igqis
waírþan nutans mannē.

9 And it came to pass in
those days, that Jesus came
from Nazareth of Galilee,
and was baptized by John in
the Jordan.
10 And straightway coming
up out of the water, he saw
the heavens opened, and the
Spirit like a dove
descending upon him:
11 And there came a voice
from heaven, saying, Thou
art my beloved Son, in
whom I am well pleased.
12 And immediately the
spirit driveth him into the
wilderness.
13 And he was there in the
wilderness forty days,
tempted of Satan; and was
with the wild beasts; and
the angels ministered unto
him.
14 Now after that John
was put in prison, Jesus
came into Galilee, preaching
the gospel of the kingdom of
God,
15 And saying, The time is
fulfilled, and the kingdom of
God is at hand: repent ye,
and believe the gospel.
16 Now as he walked by the
sea of Galilee, he saw Simon
and Andrew his brother
casting a net into the sea:
for they were fishers.
17 And Jesus said unto
them, Come ye after me,
and I will make you to
become fishers of men.

18 Yah suns aflētandans þō
natya seina láistidēdun afar
imma.
19 Yah yáinþrō inn
gaggands framis leitilata
gasaƕ Iakōbu þana
Zaíbaídaiáus yah Iōhannē
broþar is, yah þans in skipa
manwyandans natya.
20 Yah suns haíháit ins,
yah aflētandans attan
seinana Zaíbaídaiu in
þamma skipa miþ asnyam,
galiþun afar imma.
21 Yah galiþun in
Kafarnaum, yah suns
sabbatō daga galeiþands in
synagōgēn láisida ins.

22 Yah usfilmans waúrþun
ana þizái láiseinái is; untē
was láisyands ins swē
waldufni
habands yah ni swaswē þái
bōkaryōs.
23 Yah was in þizái
synagōgēn izē manna in
unhráinyamma ahmin, yah
ufhrōpida
24 qiþands; fralēt, ƕa uns
yah þus, Iēsu Nazōrēnái,
qamt fraqistyan uns? Kann
þuk, ƕas þu is, sa Weiha
Guþs.

25 Yah andbáit ina Iēsus
qiþands: þahái yah usgagg
ūt us þamma, ahma
unhráinya.
26 Yah tahida ina ahma sa
unhráinya, yah hrōpyands
stibnái mikilái usiddya us
imma.

18 And straightway they
forsook their nets and
followed him.**19** And when
he had gone a little farther
thence, he saw James the
son of Zebedee, and John
his brother, who also were
in the ship mending their
nets.
20 And straightaway he
called them: and they left
their father Zebedee in the
ship with the hired servants,
and went after him.
21 And they went into
Capernaum; and
straightway on the Sabbath
day he entered into the
synagogue, and taught.
22 And they were
astonished at his doctrine:
for he taught them as one
that had authority, and not
as the scribes.
23 And there was in their
synagogue a man with an
unclean spirit, and he cried
out,
24 Saying, Let us alone;
what have we to do with
thee, thou Jesus of
Nazareth? Art thou come to
destroy us? I know thee who
thou art, the Holy One of
God.
25 And Jesus rebuked him,
saying, Hold thy peace, and
come out of him
26 And when the unclean
spirit had torn him, and
cried with a loud voice, he
came out of him.

27 Yah afsláuþnōdēdun
allái sildaleikyandans, swaei
sōkidēdun miþ sis missō
qiþandans: ƕa siyái þata?
Ƕo so láiseinō sō niuyō? Ei
miþ waldufnya yah ahmam
þáim unhráinyam anabiudiþ
yah ufháusyand imma?

28 Usiddya þan mēriþa is
suns and allans bisitands
Galeilaias.

29 Yah suns us þizái
synagōgēn usgaggandans
qēmun in garda Seimōnis
yah Andraíins miþ lakōbáu
yah lōhannēn.

30 Iþ swaíhrō Seimōnis
lag in brinnōn, yah suns
qēþun imma bi iya.
31 Yah duatgaggands
urráisida þō undgreipands
handu izōs, yah aflaílōt þō
sō brinnō suns, yah
andbahtida im.
32 Andanahtya þan
waúrþanamma, þan gasaggq
sauil, bērun du imma allans
þans ubil habandans yah
unhulþōns habandans.
33 Yah sō baúrgs alla
garunnana was at daúra.

34 Yah gaháilida managans
ubil habandans
missaleikáim saúhtim, yah
unhulþōns managōs
uswarp, yah ni fralaílōt
rōdyan þōs unhulþōns, untē
kunþēdun ina.

27 And they were all
amazed, insomuch that they
questioned among
themselves, saying, what
thing is this? What new
doctrine is this? For with
authority commandeth he
even the unclean spirits,
and they do obey him.
28 And immediately his
fame spread abroad
throughout all the region
round about Galilee.
29 And forthwith, when
they were come out of the
synagogue, they entered
into the house of Simon and
Andrew, with James and
John.
30 But Simon's wife's
mother lay sick of a fever,
and they tell him of her.
31 And he came and took
her by the hand, and lifted
her up; and immediately the
fever left her, and she
ministered to them.
32 And at evening, when
the sun did set, they
brought unto him all that
were diseased, and them
that were possessed with
devils.
33 And all the city was
gathered together at the
door.
34 And he healed many
that were sick of divers
diseases, and cast out many
devils; and suffered not the
devils to speak, because
they knew him.

35 Yah áir ūhtwōn
usstandands usiddya, yah
galáiþ ana áuþyana staþ,
yah yáinar baþ,
36 Yah galáistans waúrþun
imma Seimōn yah þái miþ
imma.
37 Yah bigitandans ina
qēþun du imma þatei allái
þuk sōkyand.

38 Yah qaþ du im, gaggam
du þáim bisunyanē háimōm
yah baúrgim, ei yah yáinar
mēryáu, untē duþē qam.

39 Yah was mēryands in
synagōgim izē and alla
Galeilaian yah unhulþōns
uswaírpands.
40 Yah qam at imma
þrūtsfill habands, bidyands
ina yah kniwam knussyands
yah qiþands du imma þatei
yabái wileis, magt mik
gahráinyan.
41 Iþ Iēsus, infeínands,
ufrakyands handu seina
attaítōk imma yah qaþ
imma, wilyáu, waírþ hráins.

42 Yah biþē qaþ þata Iēsus,
suns þata þrūtsfill afláiþ af
imma, yah hráins warþ.

43 Yah gaƕōtyands imma
suns ussandida ina,

35 And in the morning,
rising up a great while
before day, he went out, and
departed into a solitary
place, and there prayed.
36 And Simon and they that
were with him followed
after him.
37 And when they had
found him, they said unto
him, All men seek for thee.
38 And he said unto them,
Let us go into the next
towns, that I may preach
there also: for therefore
came I forth.
39 And he preached in
their synagogues
throughout all Galilee, and
cast out devils.
40 And there came a leper
to him, beseeching him, and
kneeling down to him, and
saying unto him, If thou
wilt, thou canst make me
clean.
41 And Jesus, moved with
compassion, put forth his
hand, and touched him, and
saith unto him, I will; be
thou clean.
42 And as soon as he had
spoken, immediately the
leprosy departed from him,
and he was cleansed.
43 And he straitly charged
him, and forthwith sent him
away;

44 yah qaþ du imma, saíƕ
eí mannhun ni qiþáis waíht,
ak gagg þuk silban atáugyan
gudyin, yah atbaír fram
gahráineinái þeinái þatei
anabáuþ Mōsēs du
weitwōdiþái im.

45 Iþ is usgaggands dugann
mēryan filu yah usqiþan
þata waúrd, swaswē is
yuþan ni mahta andáugyō in
baúrg galeiþan, ak ūta ana
áuþyáim stadim was, yah
iddyēdun du imma allaþrō.

CHAPTER 2

2:1 Yah galáiþ aftra in
Kafarnaum afar dagans, yah
gafrēhun þatei in garda ist.

2 Yah suns gaqēmun
managái, swaswē yuþan ni
gamōstēdun nih at daúra,
yah rōdida im waúrd.

3 Yah qēmun at imma
usliþan baírandans,
hafanana fram fidwōrim.

4 Yah ni magandans nēƕa
qiman imma faúra
manageim, andhulidēdun
hrōt þarei was Iēsus, yah
usgrabandans insáilidēdun
þata badi, yah fralaílōtun
ana þammei lag sa usliþa.

44 And saith unto him, See
thou say nothing to any
man, but go thy way, shew
thyself to the priest, and
offer for thy cleansing those
things which Moses
commanded, for a
testimony unto them.

45 But he went out, and
began to publish it much,
and to blaze abroad the
matter, insomuch that Jesus
could no more openly enter
into the city, but was
without in desert places:
and they came to him from
every quarter.

CHAPTER 2

2:1 And again he entered
into Capernaum after some
days; and it was noised that
he was in the house.

2 And straightway many
were gathered together,
insomuch that there was no
room to receive them, no,
not so much as about the
door: and he preached the
word unto them.

3 And they come unto him,
bringing one sick of the
palsy, which was borne of
four.

4 And when they could not
come nigh unto him for the
press, they uncovered the
roof where he was: and
when they had broken it up,
they let down the bed
wherein the sick of the palsy
lay.

5 Gasaíƕands þan Iēsus
galáubein izē qaþ du þamma
usliþin, barnilō, aflētanda
þus frawaúrhteis þeinōs.
6 Wēsunuh þan sumái þizē
bōkaryē yáinar sitandans
yah þagkyandans sis in
haírtam seináim;
7 Ƕa sa swa rōdeiþ
náiteinins? Ƕas mag aflētan
frawaúrhtins, niba áins
Guþ?
8 Yah suns ufkunnands
Iēsus ahmin seinamma þatei
swa þái mitōdēdun sis, qaþ
du im, duƕē mitōþ þata in
haírtam izwaráim?

9 Ƕaþar ist azētizō du
qiban þamma usliþin;
aflētanda þus frawaúrhteis
þeinōs, þáu qiþan, urreis
yah nim þata badi þeinata
yah gagg?
10 Aþþan ei witeiþ þatei
waldufni habáiþ sunus
mans ana aírþái aflētan
frawaúrhtins, qaþ du
þamma usliþin,
11 þus qiþa, urreis nimuh
þata badi þein yah gagg du
garda þeinamma.
12 Yah urráis suns yah
ushafyands badi usiddya
faúra andwaírþya alláizē,
swaswē usgeísnōdēdun allái
yah háuhidēdun
mikilyandans Guþ,
qiþandans þatei áiw swa ni
gasēƕun, háuhidēdun
mikil-yandans Guþ,
qiþandans þatei áiw swa ni
gasēƕun.

5 When Jesus saw their
faith, he said unto the sick
of the palsy, Son, thy sins be
forgiven thee.
6 But there was certain of
the scribes sitting there, and
reasoning in their
hearts,
7 Why doth this man thus
speak blasphemies? Who
can forgive sins but God
only?
8 And immediately when
Jesus perceived in his spirit
that they so reasoned within
themselves, he said unto
them, Why reason ye these
things in your hearts?
9 Whether is it easier to say
to the sick of the palsy, Thy
sins be forgiven thee; or to
say, Arise, and take up thy
bed, and walk?
10 But that ye may know
that the Son of man hath
power on earth to forgive
sins, (he saith to the sick of
the palsy,)

11 I say unto thee, Arise,
and take up thy bed, and go
thy way into thine house.
12 And immediately he
arose, took up the bed, and
went forth before them all;
insomuch that they were all
amazed, and glorified God,
saying, We never saw it on
this fashion.

13 Yah galáiþ aftra faúr
marein, yah all manageins
iddyēdun du imma, yah
láisida ins.
14 Yah ƕarbōnds gasaƕ
Laíwwi þana Alfaiáus
sitandan at mōtái yah qaþ
du imma, gagg afar mis. Yah
usstandands iddya afar
imma.
15 Yah warþ, biþē is
anakumbida in garda is, yah
managái mōtaryōs yah
frawaúrhtái
miþanakumbidēdun lēsua
yah sipōnyam is, wēsun áuk
managái yah iddyēdun afar
imma.
16 Yah þái bōkaryōs yah
Fareisaieis gasaísƕandans
ina matyandan miþ þáim
mōtaryam yah
frawaúrhtáim, qēþun du
þáim sipōnyam is, ƕa ist
þatei miþ mōtaryam yah
frawaúrhtáim matyiþ yah
driggkiþ?
17 Yah gaháusyands lēsus
qaþ du im; ni þaúrbun
swinþái lēkeis, ak þái
ubilaba habandans; ni qam
laþōn uswaúrhtans, ak
frawaúrhtans.
18 Yah wēsun sipōnyōs
lōhannis yah Fareisaieis
fastandans; yah atiddyēdun
yah qēþun du imma, duƕē
sipōnyōs Iōhannēs yah
Fareisaieis fastand, iþ þái
þeinái sipōnyōs ni fastand?

13 And he went forth again
by the sea side; and all the
multitude resorted unto
him, and he taught them.
14 And as he passed by, he
saw Levi the son of
Alphaeus sitting at the
receipt of custom, and said
unto him, Follow me. And
he arose and followed him.
15 And it came to pass,
that, as Jesus sat at meat in
his house, many publicans
and sinners sat also
together with Jesus and his
disciples: for there were
many, and they followed
him.
16 And when the scribes
and Pharisees saw him eat
with publicans and sinners,
they said unto his disciples,
how is it that he eateth and
drinketh with publicans and
sinners?

17 When Jesus heard it, he
saith unto them, they that
are whole have no need of
the physician, but they that
are sick. I came not to call
the righteous, but sinners to
repentance.
18 And the disciples of
John and of the Pharisees
used to fast: and they come
and say unto him, Why do
the disciples of John and of
the Pharisees fast, but thy
disciples fast not?

19 Yah qaþ im Iēsus, ibái
magun sunyus brūþfadis,
und þatei miþ im ist
brūþfaþs,
fastan? Swa lagga ƕeila swē
miþ sis haband brūþfad, ni
magun fastan.
20 Aþþan atgaggand dagōs
þan afnimada af im sa
brūþfaþs, yah þan fastand in
yáinamma daga.
21 Ni manna plat fanins
niuyis siuyiþ ana snagan
faírnyana; ibái afnimái
fullōn af þamma sa niuya
þamma faírnyin, yah
waírsiza gataúra waírþiþ.

22 Ni manna giutiþ wein
yuggata in balgins
faírnyans; ibái áuftō
distaírái wein þata niuyō
þans balgins yah wein
usgutniþ, yah þái balgeis
fraqistnand; ak wein
yuggata in balgins niuyans
giutand.
23 Yah warþ þaírhgaggan
imma sabbatō daga þaírh
atisk, yah dugunnun
sipōnyōs is skēwyandans
ráupyan ahsa.
24 Yah Fareisaieis qēþun
du imma, sái, ƕa táuyand
sipōnyōs þeinái sabbatim
þatei ni skuld ist?
25 Yah is qaþ du im, niu
ussuggwuþ áiw ƕa gatawida
Daweid, þan þaúrfta yah
grēdags was, is yah þái miþ
imma?

19 And Jesus said unto
them, Can the children of
the bride-chamber fast,
while the bridegroom is
with them? As long as they
have the bridegroom with
them, they cannot fast.
20 But the days will come,
when the bridegroom shall
be taken away from them,
and then shall they fast in
those days.
21 No man also seweth a
piece of new cloth on an old
garment: else the new piece
that filled it up taketh away
from the old, and the rent is
made worse.
22 And no man putteth
new wine into old bottles:
else the new wine doth burst
the bottles,
marred: but new wine must
be put into new bottles.

23 And it came to pass,
that hc wcnt through the
corn fields on the sabbath
day; and his disciples began,
as they went, to pluck the
ears of corn.
24 And the Pharisees said
unto him, Behold, why do
they on the sabbath day that
which is not lawful?
25 And he said unto them,
Have ye never read what
David did, when he had
need, and was an hungred,
he, and they that were with
him?

26 Ƕáiwa galáiþ in gard
Gudis uf Abiaþara gudyin
yah hláibans faúrlageináis
matida, þanzei ni skuld ist
matyan niba áináim
gudyam, yah gaf yah þáim
miþ sis wisandam?

27 Yah qaþ im, sabbatō in
mans warþ gaskapans, ni
manna in sabbatō dagis;
28 swaei fráuya ist sa
sunus mans yah þamma
sabbatō.

26 How he went into the
house of God in the days of
Abiathar the high priest,
and did eat the shewbread,
which is not lawful to eat
but for the priests, and gave
also to them which were
with him?
27 And he said unto them,
The sabbath was made for
man, and not man for the
sabbath.
28 Therefore the Son of
man is Lord also of the
sabbath.

CHAPTER 3

3:1 Yah galáiþ aftra in
synagōgēn, yah was yáinar
manna gaþaúrsana habands
handu.
2 Yah witáidēdun imma
háilidēdiu sabbatō daga, ei
wrōhidēdeína ina.

3 Yah qaþ du þamma mann
þamma gaþaúrsana
habandin handu, urreis in
midumái.
4 Yah qaþ du im, skuldu ist
in sabbatim þiuþ táuyan
aíþþáu unþiuþ táuyan,
sáiwala nasyan aíþþáu
usqistyan? Iþ eis
þaháidēdun.
.

CHAPTER 3

3:1 And he entered again
into the synagogue; and
there was a man there
which had a withered hand.
2 And they watched him,
whether he would heal him
on the sabbath day; that
they might accuse him.
3 And he saith unto the
man which had the withered
hand, Stand forth.

4 And he saith unto them,
Is it lawful to do good on the
sabbath days, or to do evil?
to save life, or to kill? But
they held their peace.

5 Yah ussaíhvands ins miþ mōda, gáurs in dáubiþos haírtins izē qaþ du þamma mann, ufrakei þō handu þeína! Yah ufrakida, yah gastōþ aftra sō handus is.

6 Yah gaggandans þan Fareisaieis sunsáiw miþ þáim Hērōdianum garūni gatawidēdun bi ina, ei imma usqēmeina.

7 Yah Iēsus afláiþ miþ sipōnyam seináim du marein, yah filu manageins us Galeilaia láistidēdun afar imma,

8 yah us Iudaia yah us Iaírusaúlymim yah us Idumaia yah hindana Iaúrdanáus; yah þái bi Tyra yah Seidōna, manageins filu, gaháusyandans ƕan filu is tawida, qēmun at imma.
9 Yah qaþ þáim sipōnyam seináim ei skip habáiþ wēsi at imma in þizōs manageins, ei ni þraíheina ina.

10 Managans áuk gaháilida, swaswē drusun ana ina ei imma attaítōkeina, yah swa managái swē habáidēdun wundufnyos.

5 And when he had looked round about on them with anger, being grieved for the hardness of their hearts, he saith unto the man, Stretch forth thine hand. And he stretched it out: and his hand was restored whole as the other.
6 And the Pharisees went forth, and straightway took counsel with the Herodians against him, how they might destroy him.
7 But Jesus withdrew himself with his disciples to the sea: and a great multitude from Galilee followed him, and from Judaea,
8 And from Jerusalem, and from Idumaea, and from beyond Jordan; and they about Tyre and Sidon, a great multitude, when they had heard what great things he did, came unto him.

9 And he spake to his disciples, that a small ship should wait on him because of the multitude, lest they should throng him.
10 For he had healed many; insomuch that they pressed upon him for to touch him, as many as had plagues.

11 yah ahmans unhráinyans, þáih þan ina gasēƕun, drusun du imma yah hrōpidēdun, qiþandans, þatei þu is sunus Gudis.
12 Yah filu andbáit ins ei ina ni gaswikunþidēdeina.

13 Yah ustáig in faírguni yah athaíháit þanzei wilda is, yah galiþun du imma.

14 Yah gawaúrhta twalif du wisan miþ sis, yah ei insandidēdi ins mēryan,

15 yah haban waldufni du háilyan saúhtins yah uswaírpan unhulþōns,
16 yah gasatida Seimōna namō Paítrus,
17 yah lakōbáu þamma Zaíbaídaiáus, yah lōhannē brōþr lakōbáus, yah gasatida im namna Baúanaírgaís, þatei ist, sunyus þeihvons,
18 yah Andraían yah Filippu yah Barþaúlaúmaiu yah Matþaiu yah Þoman yah lakōbu þana Alfaiáus, yah Þaddaiu yah Seimōna þana Kananeitēn,
19 yah ludan Iskariōtēn, saei yah galēwida ina.

20 Yah atiddyēdun in gard, yah gaïddya sik *aftra* managei, swaswē ni mahtēdun nih hláif matyan.

11 And unclean spirits, when they saw him, fell down before him, and cried, saying, Thou art the Son of God.
12 And he straitly charged them that they should not make him known.
13 And he goeth up into a mountain, and calleth unto him whom he would: and they came unto him.
14 And he ordained twelve, that they should be with him, and that he might send them forth to preach,
15 And to have power to heal sicknesses, and to cast out devils:
16 And Simon he surnamed Peter;
17 And James the son of Zebedee, and John the brother of James; and he surnamed them Boanerges, which is, The sons of thunder:
18 And Andrew, and Philip, and Bartholomew, and Matthew, and Thomas, and James the son of Alphaeus, and Thaddaeus, and Simon the Canaanite,
19 And Judas Iscariot, which also betrayed him: and they went into an house.
20 And the multitude cometh together again, so that they could not so much as eat bread.

21 Yah háusyandans fram
imma bōkaryōs yah anþarái
usiddyēdun gahaban ina,
qēþun auk þatei usgáisiþs
ist.
22 Yah bōkaryōs þái af
laírusaúlymái qimandans
qēþun þatei Baíaílzaíbul
habáiþ, yah þatei in þamma
reikistin unhulþōnō
uswaírpiþ þáim unhulþōm.
23 Yah atháitands ins in
gayukōm qaþ du im: ƕáiwa
mag Satanas Satanan
uswaírpan?
24 Yah yabái þiudangardi
wiþra sik gadáilyada, ni mag
standan so þiudangardi
yáina.
25 Yah yabái gards wiþra
sik gadáilyada, ni mag
standan sa gards yáins.
26 Yah yabái Satana usstōþ
ana sik silban yah gadáiliþs
warþ, ni mag gastandan, ak
andi habáiþ.

27 Ni manna mag kasa
swinþis galeiþands in gard
is wilwan, niba faúrþis þana
swinþan
gabindiþ, yah *þan* þana gard
is diswilwái.
28 Amen, qiþa izwis, þatei
allata aflētada þata
frawaúrhtē sunum mannē,
yah náiteinōs swa managōs
swaswē wayamēryand,

29 aþþan saei wayamēreiþ
ahman weihana ni habáiþ
fralēt áiw, ak skula ist
áiweináizōs frawaúrhtáis.

21 And when his friends
heard of it, they went out to
lay hold on him: for they
said, He is beside himself.
22 And the scribes which
came down from Jerusalem
said, He hath Beelzebub,
and by the prince of the
devils casteth he out devils.

23 And he called them unto
him, and said unto them in
parables, How can Satan
cast out Satan?

24 And if a kingdom be
divided against itself, that
kingdom cannot stand.
25 And if a house be
divided against itself, that
house cannot stand.

26 And if Satan rise up
against himself, and be
divided, he cannot stand,
but hath an end.

27 No man can enter into a
strong man's house, and
spoil his goods, except he
will first bind the strong
man; and then he will spoil
his house.
28 Verily I say unto you,
All sins shall be forgiven
unto the sons of men, and
blasphemies wherewith
soever they shall
blaspheme:
29 But he that shall
blaspheme against the Holy
Ghost hath never
forgiveness, but is in danger
of eternal damnation.

30 Untē qēþun, ahman
unhráinyana habáiþ.
31 Yah qēmun þan áiþei is
yah brōþryus is yah ūta
standandōna insandidēdun
du imma, háitandōna ina.
32 Yah sētun bi ina
managei; qēþun þan du
imma: sái, áiþei þeina yah
brōþryus þeinái yah
swistryus þeinōs ūta
sōkyand þuk.
33 Yah andhōf im qiþands,
ƕo ist so áiþei meina aíþþáu
þai brōþryus meinái?
34 Yah bisaíƕands
bisunyanē þans bi sik
sitandans qaþ, sái, áiþei
meina yah þái brōþryus
meinái.
35 Saei allis waúrkeiþ
wilyan Gudis, sa yah brōþar
meins yah swistar yah áiþei
ist.

30 Because they said, He
hath an unclean spirit.
31 There came then his
brethren and his mother,
and, standing without, sent
unto him, calling him.
32 And the multitude sat
about him, and they said
unto him, Behold, thy
mother and thy brethren
without seek for thee.
33 And he answered them,
saying, Who is my mother,
or my brethren?
34 And he looked round
about on them which sat
about him, and said, Behold
my mother and my
brethren!
35 For whosoever shall do
the will of God, the same is
my brother, and my sister,
and mother.

Chapter 4

4:1 Yah aftra Iēsus dugann
láisyan at marein, yah
galēsun sik du imma
manageins filu, swaswē ina
galeiþan*dan* in skip gasitan
in marein; yah alla so
managei wiþra marein ana
staþa was.

2 Yah láisida ins in
gayukōm manag, yah qaþ
im in láiseinái seinái,
3 háuseiþ! Sái, urrann sa
saiands du saian fráiwa
seinamma.

Chapter 4

4:1 And he began again to
teach by the sea side: and
there was gathered unto
him a great multitude, so
that he entered into a ship,
and sat in the sea; and the
whole multitude was by the
sea on the land.

2 And he taught them
many things by parables,
and said unto them in his
doctrine,
3 Hearken; Behold, there
went out a sower to sow.

4 Yah warþ, miþþanei
saísō, sum raíhtis gadráus
faúr wig, yah qēmun fuglōs
yah frētun þata.
5 Anþaruþ-þan gadráus ana
stáinahamma,þarei ni
habáida aírþa managa, yah
suns urrann, in þizei ni
habáida diupáizōs aírþōs,

6 at sunnin þan
urrinnandin ufbrann, yah
untē ni habáida waúrtins
gaþaúrsnōda.
7 Yah sum gadráus in
þaúrnuns; yah ufarstigun
þái þaúrnyus yah
afƕapidēdun þata, yah
akran ni gaf.
8 Yah sum gadráus in aírþa
gōda, yah gaf akran
urrinnandō yah wahsyandō,
yah bar áin ·l· yah áin ·y·
yah áin ·r· .
9 Yah qaþ: saei habái
ausōna háusyandōna,
gaháusyái.
10 Iþ biþē warþ sundrō,
frēhun ina þái bi ina miþ
þáim twalibim þizōs
gayukōns.
11 Yah qaþ im, izwis
atgiban íst kunnan rúna
þiudangardyōs Gudis, iþ
yáináim þáim ūta in
gayukōm allata waírþiþ,

12 Ei saíƕandans saíƕáina,
yah ni gáumyáina, yah
háusyandans háusyáina yah
ni fraþyáina, nibái ƕan
gawandyáina sik yah
aflētáindáu im frawaúrhteis.

4 And it came to pass, as he
sowed, some fell by the way
side, and the fowls of the air
came and devoured it up.
5 And some fell on stony
ground, where it had not
much earth; and
immediately it sprang up,
because it had no depth of
earth:
6 But when the sun was up,
it was scorched; and
because it had no root, it
withered away.
7 And some fell among
thorns, and the thorns grew
up, and choked it, and it
yielded no fruit.
8 And other fell on good
ground, and did yield fruit
that sprang up and
increased; and brought
forth,some thirty, and some
sixty, and some an hundred.
9 And he said unto them,
He that hath ears to hear,
let him hear.
10 And when he was alone,
they that were about him
with the twelve asked of him
the parable.
11 And he said unto them,
Unto you it is given to know
the mystery of the kingdom
of God; but unto them that
are without, all these things
are done in parables.
12 That, seeing they may
see, and not perceive; and
hearing they may hear, and
not understand; lest at any
time they should be
converted, and their sins
should be forgiven them.

13 Yah qaþ du ím, ni wituþ
þō gayukōn, yah ƕáiwa allōs
þōs gayukōns kunneiþ?

14 Sa saiyands waúrd
saiyiþ.
15 Aþþan þái wiþra wig
sind, þarei saiada þata
waúrd, yah þan gaháusyand
unkaryans, suns qimiþ
Satanas yah usnimiþ waúrd
þata insaianō in haírtam izē.

16 Yah *þái* sind samaleikō
þái ana stáinahamma
saianans, þáiei þan
háusyand þata waúrd, suns
miþ fahēdái nimand ita,
17 yah ni haband waúrtins
in sis, ak ƕeilaƕaírbái sind,
þaþrōh, biþē qimiþ aglo
aíþþáu wrakya in þis
waúrdis, suns gamarzyanda.

18 Yah þái sind þái in
þaúrnuns saianans, þái
waúrd háusyandans,

19 yah saúrgōs þizōs
libáináis yah afmarzeins
gabeins yah þái bi þata
anþar lustyus inn
atgaggandans aíƕapyand
þat waúrd yah akranaláus
waírþiþ.
20 Yah þái sind þái ana
aírþái þizái gōdōn saianans
þáiei háusyand þata waúrd
yah andnimand, yah akran
baírand, áin ·l· yah áin ·y·
yah áin ·r· .

13 And he said unto them,
Know ye not this parable?
and how then will ye know
all parables?
14 The sower sows the
word.
15 And these are they by
the way side, where the
word is sown, but when they
have heard, Satan cometh
immediately, and taketh
away the word that was
sown in their hearts.
16 And these are they
likewise which are sown on
stony ground; who, when
they have heard the word,
immediately receive it with
gladness;
17 And have no root in
themselves, and so endure
but for a time: afterward,
when affliction or
persecution ariseth for the
word's sake, immediately
they are offended.
18 And these are they
which are sown among
thorns; such as hear the
word,
19 And the cares of this
world, and the deceitfulness
of riches, and the lusts of
other things entering in,
choke the word, and it
becometh unfruitful.
20 And these are they
which are sown on good
ground; such as hear the
word, and receive it, and
bring forth fruit, some
thirtyfold, some sixty, and
some an hundred.

21 Yah qaþ du im, ibái
lukarn qimiþ duþē ei uf
mēlan satyáidáu aíþþáu
undar ligr? Niu ei ana
lukarnastaþan satyáidáu?
22 Nih allis ist ƕa fulginis
þatei ni gabaírhtyáidáu, níh
warþ analáugn, ak ei
swikunþ walrþái.

23 Yabái ƕas habái áusōna
háusyandōna, gaháusyái.
24 Yah qaþ du im, saíƕiþ
ƕa háuseiþ! In þizáiei mitaþ
mitiþ, mitada izwis yah
biáukada izwis þáim
galáubyandam.

25 Untē þisƕammēh saei
habáiþ gibada imma; yah
saei ni habáiþ yah þatei
habáiþ afnimada imma.

26 Yah qaþ, swa ist
þiudangardi Gudis, swaswē
yabái manna waírpiþ fráiwa
ana aírþa.
27 Yah slēpiþ yah urreisiþ
naht yah daga, yah þata
fráiw keiniþ yah líudiþ swē
ni wait is.
28 Silbō auk aírþa akran
baíriþ: frumist gras, þaþrōh
ahs, þaþrōh fulleiþ kaúrnis
in þamma ahsa.
29 þanuh biþē atgibada
akran, suns insandeiþ gilþa,
untē atist asans.

21 And he said unto them,
Is a candle brought to be
put under a bushel, or
under a bed? and not to be
set on a candlestick?
22 For there is nothing hid,
which shall not be
manifested; neither was
anything kept secret, but
that it should come abroad.
23 If any man has ears to
hear, let him hear.
24 And he said unto them,
take heed what ye hear: with
what measure ye mete, it
shall be measured to you:
and unto you that hear shall
more be given.
25 For he that hath, to him
shall be given: and he that
hath not, from him shall be
taken even that which he
hath.
26 And he said, So is the
kingdom of God, as if a man
should cast seed into the
ground;
27 And should sleep, and
rise night and day, and the
seed should spring and grow
up, he knoweth not how.
28 For the earth bringeth
forth fruit of herself; first
the blade, then the ear, after
that the full corn in the ear.
29 But when the fruit is
brought forth, immediately
he putteth in the sickle,
because the harvest is come.

30 Yah qaþ, ƕē galeikōm
þiudangardya Gudis, aíþþáu
in ƕileikái gayukōn
gabaíram þō.

31 Swē kaúrnō sinapis,
þatei þan saiada ana aírþa,
minnist alláizē fráiwē ist
þizē ana aírþái,
32 yah þan saiada, urrinniþ
yah waírþiþ alláizē grasē
máist, yah gatáuyiþ astans
mikilans, swaswē magun uf
skadáu is fuglōs himinis
gabauan.

33 Yah swaleikáim
managáim gayukōm rōdida
du im þata waúrd, swaswē
mahtēdun háusyōn.

34 Iþ inuh gayukōn ni
rōdida im, iþ sundrō
sipōnyam seináim andband
allata.

35 Yah qaþ du im in
yáinamma daga at
andanahtya þan
waúrþanamma, usleiþam
yáinis stadis.
36 Yah aflētandans þō
managein andnēmun ina
swē was in skipa. Yah þan
anþara skipa wēsun miþ
imma.
37 Yah warþ skūra windis
mikila yah wēgōs
waltidēdun in skip, swaswē
ita yuþan gafullnōda.

30 And he said, Whereunto
shall we liken the kingdom
of God? or with what
comparison shall we
compare it?
31 It is like a grain of
mustard seed, which, when
it is sown in the earth, is less
than all the seeds that be in
the earth:
32 But when it is sown, it
groweth up, and becometh
greater than all herbs, and
shooteth out great
branches; so that the fowls
of the air may lodge under
the shadow of it.
33 And with many such
parables spake he the word
unto them, as they were
able to hear it.
34 But without a parable
spake he not unto them: and
when they were alone, he
expounded all things to his
disciples.
35 And the same day, when
the even was come, he saith
unto them, Let us pass over
unto the other side.

36 And when they had sent
away the multitude, they
took him even as he was in
the ship. And there were
also with him other little
ships.
37 And there arose a great
storm of wind, and the
waves beat into the ship, so
that it was now full.

38 Yah was is ana nōtin
ana waggarya slēpands, yah
urráisidēdun ina yah qēþun
du imma, láisari, niu kara
þuk þizei fraqistnam?

39 Yah urreisands gasōk
winda yah qaþ du marein,
gaslawái, afdumbn! Yah
anasiláida sa winds yah
warþ wis mikil.

40 Yah qaþ du im, duƕē
faúrhtái siyuþ swa? Ƕáiwa
ni naúh habáiþ galáubein?
41 Yah ohtedun sis agis
mikil, yah qethun du sis
misso, ƕas þannu sa siyai,
unte yah winds yah marei
ufhausyand imma?

38 And he was in the
hinder part of the ship,
asleep on a pillow: and they
awake him, and say unto
him, Master, carest thou not
that we perish?
39 And he arose, and
rebuked the wind, and said
unto the sea, Peace, be still.
And the wind ceased, and
there was a great calm.

40 And he said unto them,
Why are ye so fearful? How
is it that ye have no faith?
41 And they feared
exceedingly, and said one to
another, What manner of
man is this, that even the
wind and the sea obey him?

CHAPTER 5

5:1
Yah qemun hindar marein
in landa Gadarene.

2 Yah usgaggandin imma us
skipa suns gamōtida imma
manna us aúrahyōm in
ahmin unhráinyamma.

3 Saei bauáin habáida in
aúrahyōm, yah ni
náudbandyōm eisarneináim
manna mahta ina gabindan

CHAPTER 5

5:1 And they came over
unto the other side of the
sea, into the country of the
Gadarenes
2 And when he was come
out of the ship, immediately
there met him out of the
tombs a man with an
unclean spirit,
3 Who had his dwelling
among the tombs; and no
man could bind him, no, not
with chains:

4 Untē is ufta eisarnam bi
fōtuns gabuganáim yah
náudibandyōm
eisarneináim gabundans
was yah galáusida af sis þōs
náudibandyōs yah þō ana
fōtum eisarna gabrak, yah
manna ni mahta ina
gatamyan.
5 Yah sinteinō nahtam yah
dagam in aúrahyom yah in
faírgunyam was hrōpyands
yah bliggwands sik stáinam.
6 Gasaiƕands þan Iēsu
faírraþrō rann yah inwáit
ina,
7 yah hrōpyands stibnái
mikilái qaþ, ƕa mis yah þus,
Iēsu, sunáu Gudis þis
háuhistins? Biswara þuk bi
Guda, ni balwyáis mis!

8 Untē qaþ imma, usgagg,
ahma unhráinya, us þamma
mann!
9 Yah frah ina, ƕa namō
þein? Yah qaþ du imma,
namō mein Laígaíon, untē
managái siyum.
10 Yah baþ ina filu ei ni
usdrēbi im us landa.

11 Wasuh þan yáinar hairda
sweinē haldana at þamma
faírgunya.
12 Yah bēdun ina allōs þōs
unhulþōns qiþandeins,
insandei unsis in þō sweina,
ei in þō galeiþáima.

4 Because that he had been
often bound with fetters and
chains, and the chains had
been plucked asunder by
him, and the fetters broken
in pieces: neither could any
man tame him.

5 And always, night and
day, he was in the
mountains, and in the
tombs, crying, and cutting
himself with stones.
6 But when he saw Jesus
afar off, he ran and
worshipped him.
7 And cried with a loud
voice, and said, What have I
to do with thee, Jesus, thou
Son of the most high God? I
adjure thee by God, that
thou torment me not.
8 For he said unto him,
Come out of the man, thou
unclean spirit.
9 And he asked him, What
is thy name? And he
answered, saying, My name
is Legion: for we are many.
10 And he besought him
much that he would not
send them away out of the
country.
11 Now there was there
nigh unto the mountains a
great herd of swine feeding.
12 And all the devils
besought him, saying, Send
us into the swine, that we
may enter into them.

13 Yah usláubida im Iēsus
suns. Yah usgaggandans
ahmans þái unhráinyans
galiþun in þō sweina, yah
rann sō haírda and driusōn
in marein; wēsunuþ-þan
swē twōs þūsundyōs, yah
afƕapnōdēdun in marein.

14 Yah þái haldandans þō
sweina gaþlaúhun yah
gataíhun in baúrg yah in
háimōm, yah qēmun saiƕan
ƕa wēsi þata waúrþanō.
15 Yah atiddyēdun du Iēsua
yah gasaiƕand þana wōdan
sitandan yah gawasidana
yah fraþyandan þana saei
habáida laígaíon, yah
ōhtēdun.
16 Yah spillōdēdun im þáiei
gasēƕun, ƕáiwa warþ bi
þana wodan yah bi þō
sweina.

17 Yah dugunnun bidyan
ina galeiþan hindar markōs
seinōs.
18 Yah inngaggandan ina
in skip baþ ina, saei was
wōds, ei miþ imma wēsi.

19 Yah ni laílōt ina, ak qaþ
du imma, gagg du garda
þeinamma du þeináim yah
gateih im, ƕan filu þus
fráuya gatawida yah
gaarmáida þuk.

13 And forthwith Jesus
gave them leave. And the
unclean spirits went out,
and entered into the swine:
and the herd ran violently
down a steep place into the
sea, (they were about two
thousand;) and were choked
in the sea.
14 And they that fed the
swine fled, and told it in the
city, and in the country. And
they went out to see what it
was that was done.
15 And they come to Jesus,
and see him that was
possessed with the devil and
had the legion, sitting, and
clothed, and in his right
mind: and they were afraid.
16 And they that saw it told
them how it befell to him
that was possessed with the
devil, and also concerning
the swine.
17 And they began to pray
him to depart out of their
coasts.
18 And when he was come
into the ship, he that was
possessed with the devil
prayed that he might be
with him.
19 Howbeit Jesus suffered
him not, but saith unto him,
Go home to thy friends, and
tell them how great things
the Lord has done for thee,
and has had compassion on
thee.

20 Yah galáiþ yah dugann
mēryan in Daíkapaúlein,
ƕan filu gatawida imma
Iēsus, yah allái
sildaleikidēdun.
21 Yah usleiþandin Iēsua
in skipa aftra hindar
marein, gaqēmun sik
manageins filu du imma,
yah was faúra marein.

22 Yah sái, qimiþ áins þizē
swnagōgafadē namin
Yaeirus, yah saíƕands ina
gadraus du fōtum Iēsuis,
23 yah baþ ina filu, qiþands
þatei daúhtar meina
aftumist habáiþ, ei qimands
lagyáis ana þō handuns, ei
ganisái yah libái.

24 Yah galáiþ miþ imma,
yah iddyēdun afar imma
manageins filu yah þraíhun
ina.

25 Yah qinōnō suma
wisandei in runa blōþis yēra
twalif,
26 yah manag gaþulandei
fram managáim lēkyam yah
fraqimandei allamma
seinamma yah ni waíhtai
bōtida, ak máis wairs
habáida,
27 gaháusyandei bi Iesu,
atgaggandei in managein
aftana attaítōk wastyái is.

28 Untē qaþ þatei yabái
wastyōm is attēka, ganisa.

20 And he departed, and
began to publish in
Decapolis how great things
Jesus had done for him, and
all men marvel.
21 And when Jesus was
passed over again by ship
unto the other side, much
people gathered unto him:
and he was nigh unto the
sea.
22 And, behold, there
cometh one of the rulers of
the synagogue, Jairus by
name; and when he saw
him, he fell at his feet,
23 And besought him
greatly, saying, My little
daughter lieth at the point
of death: I pray thee,
come and lay thy hands on
her, that she may healed;
and she shall live.
24 And Jesus went with
him; and much people
followed him, and thronged
him.
25 And a certain woman,
which had an issue of blood
twelve years,
26 And had suffered many
things of many physicians,
and had spent all that she
had, and was nothing
bettered, but rather grew
worse,
27 When she had heard of
Jesus, came in the press
behind, and touched his
garment.
28 For she said, If I may
touch but his clothes, I shall
be whole.

29 Yah sunsáiw
gaþaúrsnōda sa brunna
blōþis izōs, yah ufkunþa ana
leika þatei gaháilnōda af
þamma slaha.
30 Yah sunsáiw Iēsus
ufkunþa in sis silbin þō us
sis maht usgaggandein;
gawandyands sik in
managein qaþ, ƕas mis
taítōk wastyōm?

31 Yah qēþun du imma
sipōnyōs is, saíƕis þō
managein þreihandein þuk
yah qiþis, ƕas mis taitōk?
32 Yah wláitōda saíƕan þō
þata táuyandein.

33 Iþ sō qinō ōgandei yah
reirandei, witandei þatei
warþ bi iya, qam yah dráus
du imma yah qaþ imma alla
þō sunya.

34 Iþ is qaþ du izái,
daúhtar, galáubeins þeina
ganasida þuk, gagg in
gawaírþi yah siyáis háila af
þamma slaha þeinamma.
35 Naúhþanuh imma
rōdyandin qēmun fram
þamma swnagōgafada,
qiþandans þatei daúhtar
þeina gaswalt, ƕa þanamáis
draibeis þana láisari?
36 Iþ Iēsus sunsáiw
gaháusyands þata wáurd
rōdiþ, qaþ du þamma
swnagōgafada, ni fáurhtei,
þatáinei galáubei.

29 And straightway the
fountain of her blood was
dried up; and she felt in her
body that she was healed of
that plague.
30 And Jesus, immediately
knowing in himself that
virtue had gone out of him,
turned him about in the
press, and said, Who
touched my clothes?
31 And his disciples said
unto him, Thou seest the
multitude thronging thee,
and sayest thou, Who
touched me?
32 And he looked round
about to see her that had
done this thing.
33 But the woman fearing
and trembling, knowing
what was done in her, came
and fell
down before him, and told
him all the truth.
34 And he said unto her,
Daughter, thy faith hath
made thee whole; go in
peace, and be whole of thy
plague.
35 While he yet spake,
there came from the ruler of
the synagogue's house
certain which said, Thy
daughter is dead: why
troublest thou the Master
any further?
36 As soon as Jesus heard
the word that was spoken,
he saith unto the synagogue
ruler, Be not afraid, only
believe.

37 Yah ni fralailōt áinohun
izē miþ sis afargaggan, nibái
Páitru yah Iakōbu yah
Iōhannen broþar Iakōbis.
38 Yah galáiþ in gard þis
swnagōgafadis yah gasaƕ
áuhyōdu yah grētandans
yah wáifaírƕyandans filu.
39 Yah innatgaggands qaþ
du im, ƕa áuhyoþ yah
grētiþ? þata barn ni
gadáuþnoda, ak slēpiþ.

40 Yah bihlōhun ina. Iþ is
uswaírpands alláim ganimiþ
attan þis barnis yah áiþein
yah þans miþ sis yah galáiþ
inn þarei was þata barn
ligandō.

41 Yah faírgráip bi handáu
þata barn qaþuh du izái,
taleiþa kumei, þatei ist
gaskeiriþ; mawilō, du þus
qiþa, urreis.

42 Yah suns urráis sō mawi
yah iddya; was áuk yērē
twalibē. Yah usgeisnōdedun
faúrhtein mikilái.

43 Yah anabáuþ im filu ei
manna ni funþi þata; yah
haíháit izái giban matyan.

CHAPTER 6

37 And he suffered no man
to follow him, save Peter,
and James, and John the
brother of James.
38 And he cometh to the
house of the ruler of the
synagogue, and seeth the
tumult, and them that wept
and wailed greatly.
39 And when he came in,
he saith unto them, Why
make ye this ado, and weep?
the damsel is not dead, but
sleepeth.
40 And they laughed him
to scorn. But when he had
put them all out, he taketh
the father and the mother of
the damsel, and them that
were with him, and entereth
in where the damsel was
lying.
41 And he took the damsel
by the hand, and said unto
her, Talitha cumi; which is,
being interpreted, Damsel, I
say unto thee, arise.
42 And straightway the
damsel arose, and walked;
for she was of the age of
twelve years. And they were
astonished with a great
astonishment.
43 And he charged them
straitly that no man should
know it; and commanded
that something should be
given her to eat.

CHAPTER 6

6:1 Yah usstōþ yáinþrō yah
qam in landa seinamma,
yah láistidedun afar imma
sipōnyōs is.

2 Yah biþē warþ sabbatō,
dugann in swnagōgē
láisyan, yah managái
háusyandans
sildaleikidēdun qiþandans;
ƕaþrō þamma þata, yah ƕō
sō handugeinō sō gibanō
imma, ei mahteis swaleikōs
þáirh handuns is waírþand?

3 Niu þata ist sa timrya, sa
sunus Maryins, iþ brōþar
Iakōba*us* yah Iúsē*zis* yah
Iudins yah Seimōnis? Yah
niu sind swistryus is hēr at
unsis? Yah gamarzidái
waúrþun in þamma.
4 Qaþ þan im Iēsus þatei
nist praúfētus unswērs, niba
in gabaúrþai seinái yah in
ganiþyam yah in garda
seinamma.

5 Yah ni mahta yáinar
áinohun mahtē gatáuyan,
niba fawáim siukáim
handuns galagyands
gaháilida.
6 Yah sildaleikida in
ungaláubeináis izē yah
bitáuh weihsa bisunyanē
láisyands.
7 Yah athaíháit þans twalif
yah dugann ins insandyan
twans ƕanzuh yah gaf im
waldufni ahmane
unhráinyáizē.

6:1 And he went out from
thence and came into his
own country; and his
disciples follow him.
2 And when the sabbath
day was come, he began to
teach in the synagogue: and
many hearing him were
astonished, saying, From
whence hath this man these
things? and what wisdom is
this which is given unto
him, that even such mighty
works are wrought by his
hands?
3 Is not this the carpenter,
the son of Mary, the brother
of James, and Joses, and of
Juda, and Simon? and are
not his sisters here with us?
And they were offended at
him.
4 But Jesus, said unto
them, A prophet is not
without honour, but in his
own country, and among his
own kin, and in his own
house.
5 And he could there do no
mighty work, save that he
laid his hands upon a few
sick folk, and healed them.
6 And he marvelled
because of their unbelief.
And he went round about
the villages, teaching.
7 And he called unto him
the twelve, and began to
send them forth by two and
two; and gave them power
over unclean spirits;

8 Yah faurbáuþ im ei waíht
ni nēmeina in wig, niba
hrugga áina, nih matibalg
nih hláif nih in gaírdos áiz,
9 ak gaskōhai sulyōm, yah
ni wasyáiþ twáim páidōm.

10 Yah qaþ du im,
þisƕaduh þei gaggáiþ in
gard, þar salyáiþ, untē
usgaggáiþ yáinþrō.

11 Yah swa managái swē ni
andnimáina izwis nih
háusyáina izwis,
usgaggandans yáinþrō
ushrisyáiþ mulda þō undarō
fōtum izwaráim du weit-
wōdiþái im. Amēn, qiþa
izwis, sutizō ist
Saúdaúmyam aiþþáu
Gaúmaúryam in daga stauōs
þáu þizái baúrg yáinái.

12 Yah usgaggandans
mēridēdun ei
idreigōdēdeina.
13 Yah unhulþōns managōs
usdribun yah gasalbōdēdun
alēwa managans siukans
yah gaháilidēdun.
14 Yah gaháusida þiudans
Hērōdēs, swikunþ allis warþ
namō is, yah qaþ þatei
Iōhannis sa dáupyands us
dáuþáim urráis, *yah* duþþē
waúrkyand þōs mahteis in
imma.

8 And commanded them
that they should take
nothing for their journey,
save a staff only; no scrip,
no bread, no money in their
purse:
9 But be shod with sandals;
and not put on two coats.

10 And he said unto them,
In what place soever ye
enter into an house, there
abide till ye depart from
that place.
11 And whosoever shall not
receive you, nor hear you,
when ye depart thence,
shake off the dust under
your feet for a testimony
against them. Verily I say
unto you, It shall be more
tolerable for Sodom and
Gomorrha in the day of
judgment, than for that city

12 And they went out and
preached that men should
repent.
13 And they cast out many
devils, and anointed with oil
many that were sick, and
healed them.
14 And king Herod heard
of him; (for his name was
spread abroad:) and he said,
That John the Baptist was
risen from the dead, and
therefore mighty works do
shew forth themselves in
him.

15 Anþarái þan qēþun þatei
Hēlias ist, anþarai þan
qeþun þatei praúfetēs ist
swē áins þizē praúfētē.
16 Gaháusyands þan
Hērodēs qaþ þatei þammei
ik háubiþ afmaímáit
Iohannē, sa ist, sah urráis us
dáuþáim.
17 Sa áuk raíhtis Herōdes
insandyands gahabáida
Iōhannēn yah gaband ina in
karkarái in Haírōdiadins
qēnáis Filippáus brōþrs
seinis, untē þō galiugáida.
18 Qaþ áuk Iōhannēs du
Hērōda þatei ni skuld ist
þus haban qēn brōþrs
þeinis.
19 Iþ so Hērodia náiw
imma yah wilda imma
usqiman yah ni mahta;
20 unte Hērōdis ōhta sis
Iōhannēn, kunnands ina
waír garaíhtana yah
weihana, yah witáida imma
yah háusyands imma manag
gatawida yah gabauryaba
imma andháusida.
21 Yah waúrþans dags
gatils, þan Hērodis mela
gabaúrþáis seináizōs
nahtamat waúrhta þaim
maistam seinaizē yah
þúsundifadim yah þáim
frumistam Galeilaias,

15 Others said, That it is
Elias. And others said, That
it is a prophet, or as one of
the prophets.
16 But when Herod heard
thereof, he said, It is John,
whom I beheaded: he is
risen from the dead.
17 For Herod himself had
sent forth and laid hold
upon John, and bound him
in prison for Herodias' sake,
his brother Philip's wife: for
he had married her.
18 For John had said unto
Herod, It is not lawful for
thee to have thy brother's
wife.
19 Therefore Herodias had
a quarrel against him, and
would have killed him; but
she could not:
20 For Herod feared John,
knowing that he was a just
man and an holy, and
observed him; and when he
heard him, he did many
things, and heard him
gladly.
21 And when a convenient
day was come, that Herod
on his birthday made a
supper to his lords, high
captains, and chief estates
of Galilee;

22 yah atgaggandein inn
daúhtar Hērōdiadins yah
plinsyandein yah
galeikandein Hērōda yah
þáim miþanakumbyandam,
qaþ þiudans du þizái
máuyái, bidei mik þisƕizuh
þei wileis, yah giba þus.
23 Yah swōr izái þatei
þisƕah þei bidyáis mik, giba
þus und halba þiudangardya
meina.

24 Iþ si usgaggandei qaþ
du áiþein seinái, ƕis
bidyáu? Iþ si qaþ, háubidis
Iōhannis þis dáupyandins.

25 Yah atgaggandei
sunsáiw sniumundō du
þamma þiudana baþ
qiþandei, wilyáu ei mis
gibáis ana mēsa háubiþ
Iōhannis þis dáupyandins.
26 Yah gáurs waúrþans sa
þiudans in þizē áiþē yah in
þizē miþanakumbyandanē
ni wilda izái ufbrikan.

27 Yah suns insandyands
sa þiudans spaikulatur,
anabáuþ briggan háubiþ is,
iþ is galeiþands afmaimáit
imma háubiþ in karkarái,

28 yah atbar þata háubiþ is
ana mēsa yah atgaf ita þizái
máuyái, yah sō mawi atgaf
ita áiþein seinái.
29 Yah gaháusyandans
sipōnyōs is qēmun yah
usnēmun leik is yah
galagidēdun ita in hláiwa.

22 And when the daughter
of the said Herodias came
in, and danced, and pleased
Herod and them that sat
with him, the king said unto
the damsel, Ask of me
whatsoever thou wilt, and I
will give it thee.
23 And he sware unto her,
Whatsoever thou shalt ask
of me, I will give it thee,
unto the half of my
kingdom.
24 And she went forth, and
said unto her mother, What
shall I ask? And she said,
The head of John the
Baptist.
25 And she came in
straightway with haste unto
the king, and asked, saying,
I will that thou give me by
and by in a charger the head
of John the Baptist.
26 And the king was
exceeding sorry; yet for his
oath's sake, and for their
sakes which sat with him, he
would not reject her.
27 And immediately the
king sent an executioner,
and commanded his head to
be brought: and he went
and beheaded him in the
prison,
28 And brought his head in
a charger, and gave it to the
damsel: and the damsel
gave it to her mother.
29 And when his disciples
heard of it, they came and
took up his corpse, and laid
it in a tomb.

30 Yah gaïddyēdun
apaustaúleis du Iēsua yah
gataíhun imma allata yah
swa filu swē gatawidē*dun* . ..

30 And the apostles
gathered themselves
together unto Jesus, and
told him all things, both
what they had done, and
what they had taught.

6:53 . . . yah duatsniwun.

6:53 . . . And when they
had passed over, they came
into the land of Gennesaret,
and drew to the shore.

54 Yah usgaggandam im us
skipa, sunsáiw
ufkunnandans ina,
55 birinnandans all þata
gawi dugunnun ana badyam
þans ubil habandans baíran,
þadei háusidēdun ei is wēsi.
56 Yah þisƕaduh þadei
iddya in háimōs aiþþáu
baúrgs aiþþáu in weihsa,
ana gagga lagidēdun
siukans yah bēdun ina ei
þáu skáuta wastyōs is
attaítōkeina; yah swa
managái swē attaítōkun
imma, ganēsun.

54 And when they were
come out of the ship,
straightway they knew him,
55 And ran through that
whole region round about,
and began to carry about in
beds those that were sick,
where they heard he was.
56 And whithersoever he
entered, into villages, or
cities, or country, they laid
the sick in the streets, and
besought him that they
might touch if it were but
the border of his garment:
and as many as touched him
were made whole.

CHAPTER 7

CHAPTER 7

7:1 Yah gaqēmun sik du
imma Fareisaieis yah sumái
þizē bōkaryē, qimandans us
Iairusaúlwmim.
2 Yah gasaiƕandans
sumans þizē sipōnyē is
gamáinyáim handum, þat-
ist unþwahanáim,
matyandans hláibans.

7:1 Then came together
unto him the Pharisees, and
certain of the scribes, which
came from Jerusalem.
2 And when they saw some
of his disciples eat bread
with defiled, that is to say,
with unwashen, hands, they
found fault.

3 Iþ Fareisaieis yah allái
Iudaieis, niba ufta þwahand
handuns, ni matyand,
habandans anafilh þizē
sinistanē,
4 Yah af maþla niba
dáupyand ni matyand, yah
anþar ist manag þatei
andnēmun du haban,
dáupeinins stiklē yah aúrkyē
yah katilē yah ligrē.

5 Þaþrōh þan frēhun ina
þái Fareisaieis yah þái
bōkaryōs, duƕē þái
sipōnyōs þeinái ni gaggand
bi þammei anafulhun þái
sinistans, ak unþwahanáim
handum matyand hláif?
6 Iþ is andhafyands qaþ du
im þatei waíla praúfētida
Ēsaïas bi izwis þans liutans,
swē gamēliþ ist, sō managei
waírilōm mik swēráiþ, iþ
haírtō izē faírra habáiþ sik
mis.
7 Iþ swarē mik blōtand,
láisyandans láiseinins,
anabusnins mannē.

8 Aflētandans raíhtis
anabusn Gudis habáiþ þatei
anafulhun mannans,
dáupeinins aúrkyē yah
stiklē, yah anþar galeik
swaleikata manag táuyib.
9 Yah qaþ du im, waíla
inwidiþ anabusn Gudis, ei
þata anafulhanō izwar
fastáiþ.

3 For the Pharisees, and all
the Jews, except they wash
their hands oft, eat not,
holding the tradition of the
elders.
4 And when they come
from the market, except
they wash, they eat not. And
many other things there be,
which they have received to
hold, as the washing of
cups, and pots, brasen
vessels, and of tables.
5 Then the Pharisees and
scribes asked him, Why
walk not thy disciples
according to the tradition of
the elders, but eat bread
with unwashen hands?
6 He answered and said
unto them, Well hath Esaias
prophesied of you
hypocrites, as it is written,
This people honoureth me
with their lips, but their
heart is far from me.
7 Howbeit in vain do they
worship me, teaching for
doctrines the
commandments of men.
8 For laying aside the
commandment of God, ye
hold the tradition of men, as
the washing of pots and
cups: and many other such
like things ye do.
9 And he said unto them,
Full well ye reject the
commandment of God, that
ye may keep your own
tradition.

10 Mōsēs áuk raíhtis qaþ,
swērái attan þeinana yah
áiþein þeina, yah, saei ubil
qiþái attin seinamma aíþþáu
áiþein seinái, dáuþáu
afdáuþyáidáu.
11 Iþ yus qiþiþ, yabái qiþái
manna attin seinamma
aíþþáu áiþein, kaúrbān,
þatei ist máiþms, þisƕah
þatei us mis gabatnis.
12 Yah ni fralētiþ ina ni
waíht táuyan attin
seinamma aíþþáu áiþein
seinái,
13 bláuþyandans waúrd
Gudis þizái anabusnái
izwarái, þōei anafulhuþ, yah
galeik swaleikata manag
táuyiþ.
**14 Yah atháitands alla þō
managein qaþ im,** háuseiþ
mis allái yah fraþyáiþ.

15 Ni waíhts ist útaþrō
mans inngaggandō in ina
þatei magi ina gamáinyan;
ak þata út gaggandō us
mann þata ist þata
gamáinyandō mannan.
16 Yabái ƕas habái áusōna
háusyandōna, gaháusyái.
**17 Yah þan galáiþ in gard
us þizái managein, frēhun
ina sipōnyōs is bi þō
gayukōn.**

10 For Moses said, Honour
thy father and thy mother;
and, Whoso curseth father
or mother, let him die the
death.
11 But ye say, If a man shall
say to his father or mother,
It is Corban, that is to say, a
gift, by whatsoever thou
mightest be profited by me;
he shall be free.
12 And ye suffer him no
more to do ought for his
father or his mother;
13 Making the word of God
of none effect through your
tradition, which ye have
delivered: and many such
like things do ye.
**14 And when he had called
all the people unto him, he
said unto them,** Hearken
unto me every one of you,
and understand,
15 There is nothing from
without a man, that
entering into him can defile
him: but the things which
come out of him, those are
they that defile the man.
16 If any man has ears to
hear, let him hear.
**17 And when he was
entered into the house from
the people, his disciples
asked him concerning the
parable.**

18 Yah qaþ du im, swa yah yus unwitans siyuþ? Ni fraþyiþ þammei all þata ūtaþrō inn gaggandō in mannan ni mag ina gamáinyan;

19 untē ni galeiþiþ imma in halrtō, ak in wamba, yah in urrunsa usgaggiþ, gahráinieiþ allans matins?

20 Qaþuþ-þan þatei þata us mann usgaggandō þata gamáineiþ mannan.
21 Innaþrō áuk us haírtin mannē mitōneis ubilōs usgaggand; kalkinassyus, hōrinassyus, maúrþra,
22 þiubya, faíhufrikeins, unsēleins, liutei, agláitei, áugo unsēl, wayamēreins, háuhhaírtei, unwiti.

23 Þō alla ubilōna innaþrō usgaggand yah gagamáinyand mannan.
24 Yah yáinþrō usstandands galáiþ in markōs Twre yah Seidōnē, yah galeiþands in gard ni wilda witan mannan yah ni mahta galáugnyan.
25 Gaháusyandei raíhtis qinō bi ina, þizōzei habáida daúhtar ahman unhráinyana, qimandei dráus du fotum is.

18 And he saith unto them, Are ye so without understanding also? Do ye not perceive, that whatsoever thing from without entereth into the man, it cannot defile him;
19 Because it entereth not into his heart, but into the belly, and goeth out into the draught, purging all meats?

20 And he said, That which cometh out of the man, that defileth the man.
21 For from within, out of the heart of men, proceed evil thoughts, adulteries, fornications, murders,
22 Thefts, covetousness, wickedness, deceit, lasciviousness, an evil eye, blasphemy, pride, foolishness:
23 All these evil things come from within, and defile the man.
24 And from thence he arose, and went into the borders of Tyre and Sidon, and entered into an house, and would have no man know it, but he could not be hid.
25 For a certain woman, whose young daughter had an unclean spirit, heard of him, and came and fell at his feet:

26 Wasuþ-þan so qinō
háiþnō, Saúrini fwnikiska
gabaúrþái, yah baþ ina ei þō
unhulþōn
uswaúrpi us daúhtr izōs.
27 Iþ Iēsus qaþ du izái, lēt
faúrþis sada waírþan barna,
untē ni gōþ ist niman hláib
barnē yah waírpan hundam.

28 Iþ si andhōf imma yah
qaþ du imma, yái fráuya,
yah áuk hundōs undarō
biuda matyand af
draúhsnōm barnē.
29 Yah qaþ du izái, in þis
waúrdis gagg, usiddya
unhulþō us daúhtr þeinái.
30 Yah galeiþandei du
garda seinamma bigat
unhulþōn usgaggana yah þō
daúhtar ligandein ana ligra.

31 Yah aftra galeiþands af
markōm Twrē yah Seídōnē
qam at, marein Galeilaiē
miþ tweihnáim markōm
Daíkapaúlaiōs.

32 Yah bērun du imma
báudana stammana, yah
bēdun ina ei lagidēdi imma
handáu.

33 Yah afnimands ina af
managein sundrō, lagida
figgrans seinans in áusōna
imma yah spēwands attaítōk
tuggōn is,
34 yah ussaíƕands du
himina gaswōgida, yah qaþ
du imma, Aíffaþa, þaíei ist,
uslukn.

26 The woman was a Greek,
a Syrophenician by nation;
and she besought him that
he would cast forth the devil
out of her daughter.
27 But Jesus said unto her,
Let the children first be
filled: for it is not meet to
take the children's bread,
and to cast it unto the dogs.
28 And she answered and
said unto him, Yes, Lord:
yet the dogs under the table
eat of the children's crumbs.
29 And he said unto her,
for this saying go thy way;
the devil is out of thy
daughter.
30 And when she was
come to her house, she
found the devil gone out,
and her daughter laid upon
the bed.
31 And again, departing
from the coasts of Tyre and
Sidon, he came unto the sea
of Galilee, through the
midst of the coasts of
Decapolis.
32 And they bring unto
him one that was deaf, and
had an impediment in his
speech; and they beseech
him to put his hand upon
him.
33 And he took him aside
from the multitude, and put
his fingers into his ears, and
he spit, and touched his
tongue;
34 And looking up to
heaven, he sighed, and saith
unto him, Ephphatha, that
is, Be opened.

35 Yah sunsáiw
usluknōdēdun imma
hliumans yah andbundnōda
bandi tuggōns is yah rōdida
raíhtaba.
36 Yah anabáuþ im ei
mann ni qēbeina; ƕan filu is
im anabáuþ, máis þamma
eis mēridēdun,

37 yah ufarassáu sildaleikidēdun qiþandans, waíla
allata gatawida, yah
báudans gatáuyiþ
gaháusyan yah
unrōdyandans rōdyan.

CHAPTER 8

8:1 In yáináim þan dagam
aftra at filu managái
managein wisandein yah ni
habandam ƕa matidēdeina,
atháitands sipōnyans qaþuh
du im,
2 infeinōda du þizái
managein, untē yu dagans
þrins miþ mis wēsun, yah ni
haband ƕa matyáina,

3 yah yabái fralēta ins
láusqiþrans du garda izē,
ufligand ana wiga, sumái
raíhtis izē falrraþrō qēmun.

4 Yah andhōfun imma
sipōnyos is, ƕaþrō þans
mag ƕas gasōþyan hláibam
ana áubidái?

5 Yah frah ins, ƕan
managans habáiþ hláibans?
Iþ eis qēþun, sibun.

35 And straightway his ears
were opened, and the string
of his tongue was loosed,
and he spake plain.
36 And he charged them
that they should tell no
man: but the more he
charged them, so much the
more a great deal they
published it;
37 And were beyond
measure astonished, saying,
He hath done all things
well: he maketh both the
deaf to hear, and the dumb
to speak.

CHAPTER 8

8:1 In those days the
multitude being very great,
and having nothing to eat,
Jesus called his disciples
unto him, and saith unto
them,
2 I have compassion on the
multitude, because they
have now been with me
three days, and have
nothing to eat:
3 And if I send them away
fasting to their own houses,
they will faint by the way:
for divers of them came
from far.
4 And his disciples
answered him, From
whence can a man satisfy
these men with bread here
in the wilderness?
5 And he asked them, How
many loaves have ye? And
they said, seven.

6 Yah anabáub þizái
managein anakumbyan ana
aírþái, yah nimands þans
sibun hláibans yah
awiliudōnds gabrak yah
atgaf sipōnyam seináim, ei
atlagidēdeina faúr; yah
atlagidēdun faúr þō
managein.
7 Yah habáidēdun fiskans
fawans, yah þans
gaþiuþyands qaþ ei
atlagidēdeina yah þans.

8 Gamatidēdun þan yah
sadái waurþun, yah
usnēmun láibō gabrukō
sibun spwreidans.
9 Wēsunuþ-þan þái
matyandans swē fidwōr
þūsundyōs, yah fralaílōt ins.

10 Yah galáiþ sunsáiw in
skip mib sipōnyam seináim,
yah qam ana fēra Magdalan.

11 Yah urrunnun
Fareisaieis yah dugunnun
miþ sōkyan imma
sōkyandans du imma táikn
us himina, fráisandans ina.
12 Yah ufswōgyands ahmin
seinamma qaþ, ƕa þata
kuni táikn sōkeiþ? Amen,
qiþa izwis; yabái gibáidáu
kunya þamma táiknē.

13 Yah aflētands ins,
Galeiþands aftra in skip
usláiþ hindar marein.

6 And he commanded the
people to sit down on the
ground: and he took the
seven loaves, and gave
thanks, and brake, and gave
to his disciples to set before
them; and they did set them
before the people.

7 And they had a few small
fishes: and he blessed, and
commanded to set them
also before them.

8 So they did eat, and were
filled: and they took up of
the broken meat that was
left seven baskets.
9 And they that had eaten
were about four thousand:
and he sent them away.
10 And straightway he
entered into a ship with his
disciples, and came into the
parts of Dalmanutha.

11 And the Pharisees came
forth, and began to question
with him, seeking of him a
sign from heaven, tempting
him.
12 And he sighed deeply in
his spirit, and saith, Why
doth this generation seek
after a sign? Verily I say
unto you, There shall no
sign be given unto this
generation.
13 And he left them, and
entering into the ship again
departed to the other side.

14 Yah ufarmunnōdēdun
niman hláibans yah niba
áinana hláif ni habáidēdun
miþ sis in skipa.
15 Yah anabáub im qiþands,
saíƕiþ ei atsaíƕiþ ízwis þís
beistís Fareisaiē yah beistis
Hērōdis.

16 Yah þāhtēdun miþ sis
missō qibandans, untē
hláibans ni habam.

17 Yah fraþyands Iēsus qaþ
du im, ƕa þaggkeiþ untē
hláibans ni habáiþ? Ni naúh
fraþyiþ nih wittuþ, untē
dáubata habáiþ haírtō
izwar.

18 Augōna habandans ni
gasaíƕiþ, yah áusōna
habandans ni gaháuseiþ,
yah ni gamunuþ.
19 Þan þans fimf hláibans
gabrak fimf þūsundyōm,
ƕan managōs táinyōns
fullōs gabrukō usnēmuþ?
Qēþun du imma, twalif.

20 Aþþan þan þans sibun
hláibans fidwōr
þūsundyōm, ƕan managans
spwreidans fullans gabrukō
usnēmuþ? Iþ eis
qēþun,sibun.
21 Yah qaþ du im, ƕáiwa ni
natíh fraþyiþ?

22 Yah qēmun in Beþaniin,
yah bērun du imma blindan
yah bēdun ina ei imma
attaítōki.

14 Now the disciples had
forgotten to take bread,
neither had they in the ship
with them more than one
loaf.
15 And he charged them,
saying, Take heed, beware
of the leaven of the
Pharisees, and of the leaven
of Herod.
16 And they reasoned
among themselves, saying,
It is because we have no
bread.
17 And when Jesus knew it,
he saith unto them, Why
reason ye, because ye have
no bread? perceive ye not
yet, neither understand?
have ye your heart yet
hardened?
18 Having eyes, see ye not?
and having ears, hear ye
not? and do ye not
remember?
19 When I brake the five
loaves among five thousand,
how many baskets full of
fragments took ye up? They
say unto him, twelve.

20 And when the seven
among four thousand, how
many baskets full of
fragments took ye up? And
they said, seven.

21 And he said unto them,
How is it that ye do not
understand?
22 And he cometh to
Bethsaida; and they bring a
blind man unto him, and
besought him to touch him.

23 Yah faírgreipands
handu þis blindins ustáuh
ina ūtana weihsis yah
speiwands in áugōna is,
atlagyands ana handuns
seinōs, frah ina gauƕa-
sēƕi?
24 Yah ussaíƕands qaþ,
gasaíƕa mans, þateí swē
bagmans gasaíƕa
gaggandans.
25 Þaþrōh aftra galagída
handuns ana þō áugōna is
yah gatawida ina ussaíƕan;
yah aftra gasatiþs warþ yah
gasaƕ baírhtaba allans.
26 Yah insandida ina du
garda is qiþands, ni in þata
weihs gaggáis, ni mannhun
qiþáis in þamma wēhsa.
27 Yah usiddya Iēsus yah
sipōnyōs is in wēhsa
Kaisarias þizōs Filippáus,
yah ana wiga frah sipōnyans
seinans qiþands du im,
ƕana mik qiþand mans
wisan?
28 Iþ eis andhōfun,
Iōhannēn þana dáupyand,
yah anþarái Hēlian: sumáih
þan áinana praúfētē.
29 Yah is qaþ du im, aþþan
yus, ƕana mik qiþiþ wisan?
Andhafyands þan Paítrus
qaþ dn imma, þu is Xristus.
30 Yah faúrbáuþ im ei
mannhun ni qēþeina bi ina.

23 And he took the blind
man by the hand, and led
him out of the town; and
when he had spit on his
eyes, and put his hands
upon him, he asked him if
he saw ought.
24 And he looked up, saying
I see men as trees, walking.

25 After that he put his
hands again upon his eyes,
and made him look up; and
he was restored, and saw
every man clearly.

26 And he sent him away to
his house, saying, Neither
go into the town, nor tell it
to any in the town.
27 And Jesus went out, and
his disciples, into the towns
of Caesarea Philippi: and by
the way he asked his
disciples, saying unto them,
Whom do men say that I
am?
28 And they answered,
John the Baptist; but some
say, Elias; and others, One
of the prophets.
29 And he saith unto them,
But whom say ye that I am?
And Peter answereth and
saith unto him, Thou art the
Christ.
30 And he charged them
that they should tell no man
of him.

31 Yah dugann láisyan ins
þatei skal sunus mans filu
winnan yah uskiusan skulds
ist fram þáim sinistam yah
þáim aúhumistam gudyam
yah bōkaryam, yah usqiman
yah afar þrins dagans
usstandan.
32 Yah swikunþaba þata
waúrd rōdida. Yah
aftiuhands ina Paítras
dugann andbeitan ina.
33 Iþ is gawandyands sik
yah gasaíƕanđs þans
siponyans seinans andbáit
Paítru qiþands, gagg hindar
mik, Satana, untē ni fraþyis
þáim Gudis, ak þaim
mannē.

34 Yah atháitands þō
mana-gein miþ sipōnyam
seináim qaþ du im, saei wili
afar mis láistyan, inwidái sik
silban, yah nimái galgan
seinana yah láistyái mik.

35 Saei allis wili sáiwala
seina ganasyan, fraqisteiþ
izái, iþ saei fraqisteiþ
sáiwalái seinái in meina yah
in þizōs aíwaggēlyōns,
ganasyiþ þō.
36 Ƕa áuk bōteiþ mannan,
yabái gageigáiþ þana falrƕu
allana yah gasleiþeiþ sik
sáiw-alái seinái?

37 Aíbþáu ƕa gibiþ manna
inmáidein sáiwalōs
seináizōs?

31 And he began to teach
them, that the Son of man
must suffer many things,
and be rejected of the
elders, and of the chief
priests, and scribes, and be
killed, and after three days
rise again.
32 And he spake that
saying openly. And Peter
took him, and began to
rebuke him.
33 But when he had turned
about and looked on his
disciples, he rebuked Peter,
saying, Get thee behind me,
Satan: for thou savourest
not the things that be of
God, but the things that be
of men.
34 And when he had called
the people unto him with
his disciples also, he said
unto them, Whosoever will
come after me, let him deny
himself, and take up his
cross, and follow me.
35 For whosoever will save
his life shall lose it; but
whosoever shall lose his life
for my sake and the
gospel's, the same shall save
it.
36 For what shall it profit a
man, if he shall gain the
whole world, and lose his
own soul?

37 Or what shall a man give
in exchange for his soul?

38 Untē saei skamáiþ sik
meina yah waúrdē meináizē
in gabaúrþái þizái
hōrinōndein yah
frawaúrhtōn, yah sunus
mans skamáiþ sik is, þan
qimiþ in wulþáu Attins
seinis miþ aggilum þáim
weiham.

CHAPTER 9

9:1 Yah qaþ du im, amen,
qiþa izwis þatei sind sumái
þizē her standandanē, þáí
izē ni káusyand dáuþáus,
untē gasaíƕand þiudinassu
Gudis qumanana in mahtái.
2 Yah afar dagans saíhs
ganam Iēsus Paítru yah
Iakōbu yah Iōhannēn, yah
ustáuh ins ana faírguni
háuh sundrō áinans, yah
inmáidida sik in andwaírþya
izē.

3 Yah wastyōs is waúrþun
glitmunyandeins, ƕeitos
swē snáiws, swaleikōs swē
wullareis ana aírþái ni mag
gaƕeityan.
4 Yah atáugibs warþ im
Hēlias miþ Mōsē, yah wēsun
rōd-yandans miþ Iēsua.
5 Yah andhafyands Paítrus
qaþ du Iēsua, rabbei, gōþ ist
unsis her wisan, yah
gawaúrk-yam hliyans þrins,
þus áinana yah Mōsē áinana
yah áinana Hēliyin.

38 Whosoever therefore
shall be ashamed of me and
of my words in this
adulterous and sinful
generation; of him also shall
the Son of man be ashamed,
when he cometh in the glory
of his Father with the holy
angels.

CHAPTER 9

9:1 And he said unto them,
Verily I say unto you, That
there be some of them that
stand here, which shall not
taste of death, till they have
seen the kingdom of God
come with power.
2 And after six days Jesus
taketh with him Peter, and
James, and John, and
leadeth them up into an
high mountain apart by
themselves, and he was
transfigured before them.
3 And his raiment became
shining, exceeding white as
snow; so as no fuller on
earth can white them.
4 And there appeared unto
them Elias with Moses, and
they were talking with
Jesus.
5 And Peter answered and
said to Jesus, Master, it is
good for us to be here: and
let us make three
tabernacles; one for thee,
and one for Moses, and one
for Elias.

6 Ni áuk wissa ƕa rōdidēdi,
wēsun áuk usagidái.

7 Yah warþ milhma
ufarskadwyands im, yah
qam stibna us þamma
milhmin, sa ist sunus meins
sa liuba; þamma háusyáiþ.
8 Yah anaks insaíƕandans
ni þanaseiþs áinōhun
gasēƕun, alya lēsu áinana
miþ sis.

9 Dalaþ þan atgaggandam
im af þamma faírgunya,
anabáuþ im ei mannhun ni
spillō-dēdeina þatei
gasēƕun, niba biþē sunus
mans us dáuþáim usstōþi.

10 Yah þata waúrd
habáidēdun du sis missō
sōkyandans, ƕa ist þata us
dáuþáim usstandan?

11 Yah frēhun ina
qiþandans, untē qiþand þái
bōkaryos þatei Hēlias skuli
qiman faúrþis?
12 Iþ is andhafyands qaþ
du im, Hēlias swēþáuh
qimands faúrþis aftra
gabōteiþ alia; yah ƕáiwa
gamēliþ ist bi sunu mans, ei
manag winnái yah frakunþs
waírþái.
13 Akei qiþa izwis þatei yu
Hēlias qam yah
gatawidēdun imma swa filu
swē wildēdun, swaswē
gamēliþ ist bi ina.

6 For he wist not what to
say, for they were sore
afraid.
7 And there was a cloud
that overshadowed them:
and a voice came out of the
cloud, saying, This is my
beloved Son: hear him.
8 And suddenly, when they
had looked round about,
they saw no man any more,
save Jesus only with
themselves.
9 And as they came down
from the mountain, he
charged them that they
should tell no man what
things they had seen, till the
Son of man were risen from
the dead.
10 And they kept that
saying with themselves,
questioning one with
another what the rising
from the dead should mean.
11 And they asked him,
saying, Why say the scribes
that Elias must first come?

12 And he answered and
told them, Elias verily
cometh first, and restoreth
all things; and how it is
written of the Son of man,
that he must suffer many
things, and be set at nought.
13 But I say unto you, That
Elias is indeed come, and
they have done unto him
whatsoever they listed, as it
is written of him.

14 Yah qimands at
sipōnyam gasaƕ filu
manageins bi ins, yah
bōkaryans sōkyandans miþ
im.
15 Yah sunsáiw alla
manageins gasaíƕandans
ina usgeisnōdēdun, yah
durinnandans inwitun ina.
16 Yah frah þans
bōkaryans, ƕa sōkeiþ miþ
þáim?
17 Yah andhafyands áins us
þizái managein qaþ, Láisari,
brāhta sunu meinana du
þus habandan ahman
unrōdyandan,
18 yah þisƕaruh þei ina
gafāhiþ, gawaírpiþ ina, yah
ƕaþyiþ yah kriustiþ
tunþuns seinans, yah
gastaúrkniþ, yah qaþ
sipōnyam þeináim ei
usdreibeina ina, yah ni
mahtēdun.

19 Iþ is andhafyands im
qaþ, Ō kuni ungaláubyandō!
Und ƕa at izwis siyáu? Und
ƕa þuláu izwis? Baíriþ ina
du mis.
20 Yah brāhtēdun ina at
imma, yah gasaíƕands ina
sunsaíw sa ahma tahida ina,
yah driusands ana aírþa
walwisōda ƕaþyands.

21 Yah frah þana attan is,
ƕan lagg mēl ist ei þata
warþ imma? Iþ is qaþ, us
barniskya.

14 And when he came to
his disciples, he saw a great
multitude about them, and
the scribes questioning with
them.
15 And straightway all the
people, when they beheld
him, were greatly amazed,
and running to him saluted
him.
16 And he asked the
scribes, What question ye
with them?
17 And one of the multitude
answered and said, Master,
I have brought unto thee my
son, which hath a dumb
spirit;
18 And wheresoever he
taketh him, he teareth him:
and he foameth, and
gnasheth with his teeth, and
pineth away: and I spake to
thy disciples that they
should cast him out; and
they could not.
19 He answereth him, and
saith, O faithless generation,
how long shall I be with
you? How long shall I suffer
you? Bring him unto me.
20 And they brought him
unto him: and when he saw
him, straightway the spirit
tare him; and he fell on the
ground, & wallowed
foaming.
21 And he asked his father,
How long is it ago since this
came unto him? And he
said, Of a child.

22 Yah ufta ina yah in fōn
atwarp yah in watō, eí
usqistidēdi imma; akei
yabái mageis, hilp unsara,
gableiþ- yands unsis.

23 Iþ Iēsus qaþ du imma
þata yabái mageis
galáubyan, allata mahteig
þamma galáubyandin.
24 Yah sunsáiw
ufhrōpyands sa atta þis
barnis miþ tagram qaþ,
galáubya; hilp meináizōs
ungaláubeináis!
25 Gasaíƕands þan Iēsus
þatei samaþ rann managei,
gaƕōtida ahmin þamma
unhráinyin, qiþands du
imma, þu ahma, þu
unrōdyands yah báuþs, ik
þus anabiuda, usgagg us
þamma, yah þanaseiþs ni
galeiþáis in ina.
26 Yah hrōpyands yah filu
tahyands ina usiddya yah
warþ swē dáuþs, swaswē
managái qēþun þatei
gaswalt.
27 Iþ Iēsus undgreipands
ina bi handáu urráisida ina
yah usstōþ.
28 Yah galeiþandan ina in
gard, sipōnyōs is frēhun ina
sundrō; duƕē weis ni
mahtēdum usdreiban þana?
29 Yah qaþ du im, þata
kuni in waíhtái ni mag
usgaggan, niba in bidái yah
fastubnya.
30 Yah yáinþrō
usgaggandans iddyēdun
þaírh Galeilaian, yah ni
wilda ei ƕas wissēdi,

22 And ofttimes it hath cast
him into the fire, and into
the waters, to destroy him:
but if thou canst do any
thing, have compassion on
us, & help us.
23 Jesus said unto him, If
thou canst believe, all things
are possible to him that
believeth.
24 And straightway the
father of the child cried out,
and said with tears, Lord, I
believe; help thou mine
unbelief.
25 When Jesus saw that
the people came running
together, he rebuked the
foul spirit, saying unto him,
Thou dumb and deaf spirit,
I charge thee, come out of
him, and enter no more into
him.
26 And the spirit cried, and
rent him sore, and came out
of him, and he was as one
dead, insomuch that many
said, He is dead.
27 But Jesus took him by
the hand, and lifted him up
and he arose.
28 And when he was come
into the house, his disciples
asked him privately, Why
could not we cast him out?
29 And he said unto them,
This kind can come forth by
nothing but by prayer and
fasting.
30 And they departed
thence, and passed through
Galilee; and he would not
that any man should know
it.

31 untē láisida sipōnyans
seinans, yah qaþ du im þatei
sunus mans atgibada in
handuns mannē, yah
usqimand imma, yah
usqistiþs þridyin daga
usstandiþ.

32 Iþ eis ni frōþun þamma
waúrda, yah ōhtēdun ina
fraíhnan.
33 Yah qam in Kafarnaum,
yah in garda qumans frah
ins, ƕa in wiga miþ izwis
missō mitōdēduþ?
34 Iþ eis slawáidēdun; du
sis míssō andrunnun,
ƕaryis máists wēsi.

35 Yah sitands atwōpida
þans twalif yah qaþ du im,
yabái ƕas wili frumists
wisan, siyái alláizē aftumists
yah alláim andbahts.
36 Yah nimands barn
gasatida ita in midyáim im,
yah ana armins nimands ita
qaþ du im,

37 saei áin þizē swaleikáizē
barnē andnimiþ ana namin
meinamma, mik andnimiþ;
yah saƕazuh saei mik
andnimiþ, ni mik andnimiþ,
ak þana sandyandan mik.

31 For he taught his
disciples, and said unto
them, The Son of man is
delivered into the hands of
men, and they shall kill him;
and after that he is killed, he
shall rise the third day.
32 But they understood not
that saying, and were afraid
to ask him.
33 And he came to
Capernaum: and being in
the house he asked them,
What was it that ye disputed
among yourselves by the
way?
34 But they held their
peace: for by the way they
had disputed among
themselves, who should be
the greatest.
35 And he sat down, and
called the twelve, and saith
unto them, If any man
desire to be first, the same
shall be last of all, and
servant of all.
36 And he took a child, and
set him in the midst of
them: and when he had
taken him in his arms, he
said unto them,
37 Whosoever shall receive
one of such children in my
name, receiveth me: and
whosoever shall receive me,
receiveth not me, but him
that sent me.

38 Andhōf þan imma
Iōhannēs qiþands,Láisari,
sēƕum sumana in
þeinamma namin
usdreibandan unhulþōns,
saei ni láisteiþ unsis; yah
waridēdum imma, untē ni
láisteiþ unsis.
39 Iþ is qaþ, ni waryiþ
imma, ni mannahun áuk ist
saei táuyiþ maht in namin
meinamma yah magi
spráutō ubilwaúrdyan mis.
40 untē saei nist wiþra
izwís, faúr izwis ist.
41 Saei áuk allis gadragkyái
izwis stikla watins in namin
meinamma, untē Xristáus
siyuþ, amen qiþa izwis ei ni
fraqisteiþ mizdōn seinái.

42 Yah saƕazuh saei
gamarzyái áinana þizē
leitilanē þizē galáubyandanē
du mis, gōþ ist imma máis ei
galagyáidáu asiluqaírnus
ana balsaggan is yah
frawaúrpans wēsi in marein.
43 Yah yabái marzyái þuk
handus þeina, afmáit þō:
gōþ þus ist hamfamma in
libáin galeiþan, þáu twōs
handuns habandin galeiþan
in
gaíaínnan, in fōn þata
unƕapnandō,
44 þarei maþa izē ni
gaswiltiþ yah fōn ni
afƕapniþ.

38 And John answered
him, saying, Master, we saw
one casting out devils in thy
name, and he followeth not
us: and we forbad him,
because he followeth not us.

39 But Jesus said, Forbid
him not: for there is no man
which shall do a miracle in
my name, that can lightly
speak evil of me.

40 For he that is not
against us is on our part.
41 For whosoever shall give
you a cup of water to drink
in my name, because ye
belong to Christ, verily I say
unto you, he shall not lose
his reward.
42 And whosoever shall
offend one of these little
ones that believe in me, it is
better for him that a
millstone were hanged
about his neck, and he were
cast into the sea
43 And if thy hand offend
thee, cut it off: it is better
for thee to enter into life
maimed, than having two
hands to go into hell, into
the fire that never shall be
quenched:

44 Where their worm dieth
not, and the fire is not
quenched.

45 Yah yabái fōtus þeins
marzyái þuk, afmáit ina; gōþ
þus ist galeiþan in libáin
haltamma, þáu twans fotuns
habandin gawaírpan in
gaíaínnan, in fōn þata
unƕapnandō,
46 þarei maþa izē ni
gaswutiþ yah fōn ni
afƕapniþ.
47 Yah yabái áugō þein
marzyái þuk, uswaírp imma;
gōþ þus ist háihamma
galeiþan in
þiudangardya Gudis, þáu
twa áugōna habandin
atwaírpan in gaíaínnan
funins,
48 þarei maþa izē ni
gadáuþniþ yah fōn ni
afƕapniþ.
49 Ƕazuh áuk funin
saltada yah ƕaryatōh hunslē
salta saltada.
50 Gōþ salt; iþ yabái salt
unsaltan waírþiþ, ƕē
supūda? Habáiþ in izwis
salt, yah gawaírþeigái síyáiþ
miþ izwis missō.

45 And if thy foot offend
thee, cut it off: it is better
for thee to enter halt into
life, than having two feet to
be cast into hell, into the fire
that never shall be
quenched:
46 Where their worm dieth
not, and the fire is not
quenched.
47 And if thine eye offend
thee, pluck it out: it is better
for thee to enter into the
kingdom of God with one
eye, than having two eyes to
be cast into hell fire:
48 Where their worm dieth
not, and the fire is not
quenched.
49 For every one shall be
salted with fire, and every
sacrifice shall be salted with
salt.
50 Salt is good: but if the
salt have lost his saltness,
wherewith will ye season it?
Have salt in yourselves, and
have peace one with
another.

CHAPTER 10

10:1 Yah yáínþrō
usstandands qam in
markōm ludaias hindar
laúrdanáu; yah gaqēmun sik
aftra manageins du imma,
yah, swē biūhts *was,* aftra
láisida ins.

CHAPTER 10

10:1 And he arose from
thence, and cometh into the
coasts of Judaea by the
farther side of Jordan: and
the people resort unto him
again; and, as he was wont,
he taught them again.

2 Yah duatgaggandans
Fareisaieis frēhun ina,
skuldu siyái mann qēn
afsatyan, fráisandans ina.
3 Iþ is andhafyands qaþ,
ƕa izwis anabáuþ Mōsēs?

4 Iþ eis qēþun, Mōsēs
usláubida unsis bōkōs
afsateináis mēlyan yah
aflētan.

5 Yah andhafyands Iēsus
qaþ du im, wiþra
harduhaírtein izwara
gamēlida izwis þō anabusn.

6 Iþ af anastōdeinái
gaskaftáis gumein yah
qinein gatawid Guþ.
7 Inuh þis bileiþái manna
attin seinamma yah áiþein
seinái,
8 yah siyáina þō twa du
leika samin, swaswē
þanaseiþs ní sind twa, ak
leik áin.

9 Þatei nu Guþ gawaþ,
manna þamma ni skáidái.

10 Yah in garda aftra
sipōnyōs is bi þata samō
frēhun ina.
11 Yah qaþ du im, saƕazuh
saei, aflētiþ qēn seina yah
liugáiþ anþara, hōrinōþ du
þizái.

12 Yah yabái qinō aflētiþ
aban seinana yah liugada
anþaramma, hōrinōþ.

2 And the Pharisees came
to him, and asked him, Is it
lawful for a man to put away
his wife? tempting him
3 And he answered and
said unto them, What did
Moses command you?

4 And they said, Moses
suffered to write a bill of
divorcement, and to put her
away.

5 And Jesus answered and
said unto them, For the
hardness of your heart he
wrote you this precept.

6 But from the beginning of
the creation God made them
male and female.
7 For this cause shall a man
leave his father and mother,
and cleave to his wife;
8 And they twain shall be
one flesh: so then they are
no more twain, but one
flesh.
9 What therefore God hath
joined together, let not man
put asunder.
10 And in the house his
disciples asked him again of
the same matter.
11 And he saith unto them,
Whosoever shall put away
his wife, and marry another,
com-mitteth adultery
against her.
12 And if a woman shall
put away her husband, and
be married to another, she
committeth adultery.

13 þanuh atbērun du imma
barna, ei attaítōki im, iþ þái
sipōnyōs is sōkun þáim
baírandam du.

14 Gasaíƕands þan Iēsus
unwērida yah qaþ du im,
lētiþ þō barna gaggan du
mis yah ni waryiþ þō, untē
þizē ist þiudangardi
Gudis.

15 Amen, qiþa izwis; saei ni
andnimiþ þiudangardya
Gudis swē barn, ni þáuh
qimiþ in izái.

16 Yah gaþláihands im,
lagyands handuns ana þō
þiuþida im.
17 Yah usgaggandin imma
in wig, duatrinnands áins
yah knussyands baþ ina
qiþands: Láisari Þiuþeiga,
ƕa táuyáu ei libáináis
áiweinōns arbya waírþáu?

18 Iþ is qaþ du imma, ƕa
mik qiþis þiuþeigana? Ni
ƕashun þiuþeigs, alya áins
Guþ.

19 Þōs anabusnins kant: ni
hōrinōs; ni maárþryáis; ni
hlifáis; ni siyáis
galiugaweitwōds; ni
anamahtyáis; swērái attan
þeinana yah áiþein þeina.

20 þaruh andhafyands qaþ
du imma: láisari, þō alla
gafastáida us yundái meināi.

13 And they brought young
children to him, that he
should touch them: and his
disciples rebuked those that
brought them.
14 But when Jesus saw it,
he was much displeased,
and said unto them, Suffer
the little children to come
unto me, and forbid them
not: for of such is the
kingdom of God.
15 Verily I say unto you,
Whosoever shall not receive
the kingdom of God as a
littlechild, he shall not enter
therein.
16 And he took them up in
his arms, put his hands
upon them, and blessed
them.
17 And when he was gone
forth into the way, there
came one running, and
kneeled to him, and asked
him, Good Master, what
shall I do that I may inherit
eternal life?
18 And Jesus said unto
him, Why callest thou me
good? there is none good
but one, that is, God.
19 Thou knowest the
commandments, Do not
commit adultery, Do not
kill, Do not steal, Do not
bear false witness, Defraud
not, Honor thy father and
mother.
20 And he answered and
said unto him, Master, all
these have I observed from
my youth.

21 Iþ Iēsus insaíƕands du
imma friyōda ina yah qaþ
du imma; áinis þus wan ist;
gagg, swa filu swē habáis
frabugei yah gif þarbam, yah
habáis huzd in himinam;
yah hiri láistyan mik
nimands galgan.

22 Iþ is gahnipnands in þis
waúrdis galáiþ gáurs; was
áuk habands faíhu manag.
23 Yah bisaíƕands Iēsus
qaþ sipōnyam seináim, sái,
ƕáiwa agluba þái faíhō
gahabandans in
þiudangardya Gudis
galeiþand.
24 Iþ þái sipōnyōs afsláuþnōdēdun in waúrdē is.
Þaruh Iēsus aftra
andhafyands qaþ im,
barnilōna, ƕáiwa aglu ist
þáim hugyandam afar
faíháu in þiudangardya
Gudis galeiþan.
25 Azitizō ist ulbandáu
þaírh þaírkō nēþlōs
galeiþan, þáu gabigamma in
þiudangardya Gudi
galeiþan.
26 Iþ eis máis usgeisnōdēdun qiþandans du sis
missō, yah ƕas mag
ganisan?
27 Insaíƕands du im Iēsus
qaþ, *akei* fram mannam
unmahteig ist, akei ni fram
Guþa; allata áuk mahteig ist
fram Guþa.

21 Then Jesus beholding
him loved him, and said
unto him, One thing thou
lackest; go thy way, sell
whatsoever thou hast, and
give to the poor, and thou
shalt have treasure in
heaven: and come, take up
the cross, and follow me.
22 And he was sad at that
saying, and went away
grieved: for he had great
possessions.
23 And Jesus looked round
about, and saith unto his
disciples, How hardly shall
they that have riches enter
into the kingdom of God!
24 And the disciples were
astonished at his words. But
Jesus answereth again, and
saith unto them, Children,
how hard is it for them that
trust in riches to enter into
the kingdom of God!
25 It is easier for a camel to
go through the eye of a
needle, than for a rich man
to enter into the kingdom of
God.
26 And they were
astonished out of measure,
saying among themselves,
Who then can be saved?
27 And Jesus looking upon
them saith, With men it is
impossible, but not with
God: for with God all things
are possible.

28 Dugann þan Paítrus qiþan du imma, sái, weis aflaílōtum alla yah láistídēdum þuk.

29 Andhafyands im Iēsus qaþ, amen, qiþa izwis, ni ƕashun ist saei aflaílōti gard aíbþáu brōþruns *aíþþáu swistruns* aíþþáu áiþein aíþbáu attan aíþþáu qēn aíþþáu barna aíþþáu háimōþlya in meina yah in þizōs aíwaggēlyōns.

30 Saei ni andnimái ·r· falþ nu in þamma mēla gardins yah brōþruns yah swistruns attan yah áiþein yah barna yah háimōþlya miþ wrakōm, yah in áiwa þamma anawafrþin libáin áiweinōn.

31 Aþþan managái waírþand frumans aftumans, yah aftumans frumans.

32 Wēsunuþ-þan ana wiga gaggandans du Iaírusaúlwmái yah *was* faúrbigaggands ins Iēsus, yah sildaleikidēdun yah afarláistyandans faúrhtái waúrþun. Yah andnimands aftra þans twalif dugann im qiþan þōei habáidēdun ina gadaban.

33 Þatei, sái, usgaggam in Iaírusaúlwma yah sunus mans atgibada þáim ufargudyam yah bōkaryam, yah gawargyand ina dáuþáu *yah atgiband ina þiudom;*

28 Then Peter began to say unto him, Lo, we have left all, and have followed thee.

29 And Jesus answered and said, Verily I say unto you, There is no man that hath left house, or brethren, or sisters, or father, or mother, or wife, or children, or lands, for my sake, and the gospel's,

30 But he shall receive an hundredfold now in this time, houses, and brethren, and sisters, and mothers, and children, and lands, with persecutions; and in the world to come eternal life.

31 But many that are first shall be last; and the last first.

32 And they were in the way going up to Jerusalem; and Jesus went before them: and they were amazed; and as they followed, they were afraid. And he took again the twelve, and began to tell them what things should happen unto him.

33 Saying, Behold, we go up to Jerusalem; and the Son of man shall be delivered unto the chief priests, and unto the scribes; and they shall condemn him to death, and shall deliver him to the Gentiles:

34 yah biláikand ina yah
bliggwand ina yah speiwand
ana ina yah usqimand
imma, yah þridyin daga
ustandiþ.
35 Yah athabáidēdun sik
du imma Iakōbus yah
Iōhannēs, sunyus
Zaíbaídaiáus, qiþandans,
láisari, wileima ei þatei þuk
bidyōs, táuyáis uggkis.

36 Iþ Iēsus qaþ im, ƕa
wileits táuyan mik igqis?

37 Iþ eis qēþun du imma,
fragif ugkis ei ains af
taihswōn þeinái yah áins af
hleidumein þeinai sitáiwa in
wulþáu þeinamma.
38 Iþ Iēsus qaþuh du im, ni
wituts ƕis bidyats, magutsu
driggkan stikl þanei ik
driggka, yah dáupeinái
þizaiei ik dáupyada, ei
dáupyáindáu?
39 Iþ eis qēþun du imma,
magu. Iþ Iēsus qaþuh du im,
swēþáuh þana stikl þanei ik
driggka, driggkats yah þizái
dáupeinái þizáiei ik
dáupyada *dáupyanda*

40 Iþ þata du sitan af
taíhswōn meinái aíþþáu af
hleidumein nist mein du
giban, alya þáimei manwiþ
was.
41 Yah gaháusyandans þái
taíhun dugunnun unwēryan
bi Iakōbu yah Iōhannēn.

34 And they shall mock
him, and shall scourge him,
and shall spit upon him, and
shall kill him: and the third
day he shall rise again.
35 And James and John,
the sons of Zebedee, come
unto him, saying, Master,
we would that thou
shouldest do for us
whatsoever we shall desire.

36 And he said unto them,
What would ye that I should
do for you?
37 They said unto him,
Grant unto us that we may
sit, one on thy right hand,
and the other on thy left
hand, in thy glory.
38 But Jesus said unto
them, Ye know not what ye
ask: can ye drink of the cup
that I drink of? and be
baptized with the baptism
that I am baptized with?
39 And they said unto him,
We can. And Jesus said
unto them, Ye shall indeed
drink of the cup that I drink
of; and with the baptism
that I am baptized with shall
ye be baptized.
40 But to sit on my right
hand and on my left hand is
not mine to give; but it shall
be given to them for whom
it is prepared.
41 And when the ten heard
it, they began to be much
displeased with James and
John.

42 Iþ is atháitands ins qaþ
du im, wituþ þatei *þáiei*
þuggkyand reikinon
þiudōm, gafráuyinond im,
iþ þái mikilans izē
gawaldand im.

43 Iþ ni swa siyái in izwis;
ak saƕazuh saei wili
waírþan mikils in izwis,
siyái izwar andbahts;
44 yah saei wili izwara
waírþan frumists, siyái
allaim skalks.

45 Yah áuk sunus mans ni
qam at andbahtyam, ak
andbahtyan yah giban
sáiwala seina fáur
managans lun.

46 Yah qēmun in Iaírikōn.
Yah usgaggandin imma
yáinþrō miþ sipōnyam
seináim yah mana-
gein ganōhái, sunus
Teimaiáus, Barteimaiáus *sa*
blinda, sat faúr wig du
áihtron.
47 Yah gaháusyands þatei
Iēsus sa Nazōraius ist,
dugann hrōpyan yah qiþan,
sunáu Daweidis, Iēsu, armái
mik!
48 Yah ƕōtidēdun imma
managái ei gaþahaidēdi, iþ
is filu mais hrōpida, sunau
Daweidis, armái mik!
49 Yah gastandands Iēsus
haiháit atwōpyan ina. Yah
wōpidēdun þana blindan,
qiþandans du imma,
þrafstei þuk, urreis, wōpeiþ
þuk.

42 But Jesus called them to
him, and saith unto them,
Ye know that they which are
accounted to rule over the
Gentiles exercise lordship
over them; and their great
ones exercise authority
upon them.
43 But so shall it not be
among you: but whosoever
will be great among you,
shall be your minister:
44 And whosoever of you
will be the chiefest, shall be
servant of all.
45 For even the Son of man
came not to be ministered
unto, but to minister, and to
give his life a ransom for
many.
46 And they came to
Jericho: and as he went out
of Jericho with his disciples
and a great number of
people, blind Bartimaeus,
the son of Timaeus, sat by
the highway side begging

47 And when he heard that
it was Jesus of Nazareth, he
began to cry out, and say,
Jesus, thou son of David,
have mercy on me.
48 And many charged him
that he should hold his
peace: but he cried the more
a great deal, Thou son of
David, have mercy on me.
49 And Jesus stood still,
and commanded him to be
called. And they call the
blind man, saying unto him,
Be of good comfort, rise; he
calleth thee.

50 Iþ is afwaírpands
wastyái seinái ushlaupands
qam at Iēsu.
51 Yah andhafyands qaþ du
imma Iēsus, ƕa wileis ei
táuyáu þus? Iþ sa blinda
qaþ du imma, rabbaunei, ei
ussaíƕáu.

52 Iþ Iēsus qaþ du imma,
gagg, galáubeins þeina
ganasida þuk. Yah sunsáiw
ussaƕ yah láistida in wiga
Iēsu.

CHAPTER 11

11:1 Yah biþē nēƕa wesun
Iaírusalēm, in Bēþsfagein
yah Biþaniin at faírgunya
alēwyin, insandida twans
sipōnyē seináizē.
2 Yah qaþ du im, gaggats
in háim þō wiþrawaírþōn
iggqis, yah sunsáiw
inngaggandans in þō báurg
bigitats fulan gabundanana,
ana þammei nauh áinshun
mannē ni sat;
andbindandans ina
attiuhats.
3 Yah yabái ƕas iggqis
qiþái, duƕē þata táuyats?
Qiþáits þatei fráuya þis
gaírneiþ, yah sunsáiw ina
insandeiþ hidrē.
4 Galiþun þan yah bigētun
fulan gabundanana at daúra
ūta ana gagga; yah
andbundun ina.

50 And he, casting away
his garment, rose, and came
to Jesus.
51 And Jesus answered and
said unto him, What wilt
thou that I should do unto
thee? The blind man said
unto him, Lord, that I might
receive my sight.
52 And Jesus said unto
him, Go thy way; thy faith
hath made thee whole. And
immediately he received his
sight, and followed Jesus in
the way.

CHAPTER 11

11:1 And when they came
nigh to Jerusalem, unto
Bethphage and Bethany, at
the mount of Olives, he
sendeth forth two of his
disciples,
2 And saith unto them, Go
your way into the village
over against you: and as
soon as ye be entered into it,
ye shall find a colt tied,
whereon never man sat;
loose him, and bring him.

3 And if any man say unto
you, Why do ye this? say ye
that the Lord hath need of
him; and straightway he will
send him hither.
4 And they went their way,
and found the colt tied by
the door without in a place
where two ways met; and
they loose him.

5 Yah sumái þizē yáinar
standandanē qēþun du im,
ƕa táuyats andbindandans
þana fulan?
6 Iþ eis qēþun du im
swaswē anabáuþ im Iēsus,
yah laílōtun ins.

7 Yah brāhtēdun þana fulan
at Iēsua yah galagidēdun
ana *ina* wastyōs seinōs, yah
gasat ana ina.
8 Managái þan wastyōm
seináim strawidēdun ana
wiga; sumái astans
maímáitun us bagmam yah
strawidēdun ana wiga.
9 Yah þái faúragaggandans
yah þái afarlaistyandans
hrōpidēdun qiþandans,
ōsanna, þiuþida sa qimanda
in namin fráuyins!

10 Þiuþidō sō qimandei
þiudangardi in namin
frauyins attins unsaris
Daweidis, ōsanna in
háuhistyam!
11 Yah galáiþ in
Iaírusaúlwma Iēsus yah in
alh; yah bisaíƕands alla, at
andanahtya yuþan wisandin
ƕeilái usiddya in Bēþanian
miþ þáim twalibim.

12 Yah iftumin daga
usstandandam im us
Bēþaniin gredags was.

5 And certain of them that
stood there said unto them,
What do ye, loosing the
colt?
6 And they said unto them
even as Jesus had
commanded: and they let
them go.
7 And they brought the colt
to Jesus and cast their
garments on him; and he sat
upon him.
8 And many spread their
garments in the way: and
others cut down branches
off the trees, and strawed
them in the way.
9 And they that went
before, and they that
followed, cried, saying,
Hosanna; Blessed is he that
cometh in the name of the
Lord!
10 Blessed be the kingdom
of our father David, that
cometh in the name of the
Lord: Hosanna in the
highest.
11 And Jesus entered into
Jerusalem, and into the
temple: and when he had
looked round about upon all
things, and now the
eventide was come, he went
out unto Bethany with the
twelve.
12 And on the morrow,
when they were come from
Bethany, he was hungry:

13 Yah gasaíƕands
smakkabagm faírraþrō
habandan láuf atiddya, ei
áufto bigēti ƕa ana imma;
yah qimands at imma ni
waiht bigat ana imma niba
láuf; ni áuk was mēl
smakkanē.
14 Yah usbaírands qaþ du
imma, ni þanaseiþs us þus
áiw manna akran matyái.
Yah gaháusidedun þái
sipōnyōs is.
15 Yah iddyēdun du
Iaírusaulwmái. Yah
atgaggands Iēsus in alh
dugann uswaírpan þans
frabugyandans yah
bugyandans in alh yah mēsa
skattyanē yah sitlans þizē
frabugyandanē ahakim
uswaltida.
16 Yah ni lailōt ei ƕas
þaírhberi kas þaírh þō alh.

17 Yah láisida qiþands du
im, niu gamēliþ ist þatei
razn mein razn bidō háitada
alláim þiudōm? Iþ yus
gatawidēduþ ita du filigrya
wáidēdyanē.
18 Yah gaháusidēdun þái
bōkaryōs yah gudyanē
aúhumistans yah
sōkidēdun, ƕáiwa imma
usqistidedeina, ōhtedun áuk
ina, unte alla managei
sildaleikidēdun in láiseinais
is.
19 Yah biþē andanahti
warþ, usiddya ūt us þizái
baúrg.

13 And seeing a fig tree afar
off having leaves, he came,
if haply he might find any
thing thereon: and when he
came to it, he found nothing
but leaves; for the time of
figs was not yet.

14 And Jesus answered and
said unto it, No man eat
fruit of thee hereafter for
ever. And his disciples
heard it.
15 And they come to
Jerusalem: and Jesus went
into the temple, and began
to cast out them that sold
and bought in the temple,
and overthrew the tables of
the moneychangers, and the
seats of them that sold
doves;
16 And would not suffer
that any man should carry
any vessel through the
temple.
17 And he taught, saying
unto them, Is it not written,
My house shall be called of
all nations the house of
prayer? But you have made
it a den of thieves.
18 And the scribes and
chief priests heard it, and
sought how they might
destroy him: for they feared
him, because all the people
was astonished at his
doctrine.
19 And when even was
come, he went out of the
city.

20 Yah in maúrgin faúr-
gaggandans gasēƕun þana
smakkabagm þaúrsyana us
waúrtim.
21 Yah gamunands Paítrus
qaþ du imma, rabbei, sái,
smakkabagms þanei fraqast
gaþaúrsnoda.
22 Yah andhafyands Iēsus
qaþ du im, habáiþ galáubein
Gudis.

23 Amen áuk qiþa izwis,
þisƕazuh ei qiþái
du þamma faírgunya,
ushafei þuk yah wairp þus
in marein, yah ni tuzweryai
in haírtin seinamma, ak
galáubyai þata, ei þatei qiþiþ
gagaggiþ, waírþiþ imma
þisƕah þei qiþiþ.

24 Duþþē qiþa izwis, allata
þisƕah þei bidyandans
sōkeiþ, galáubeiþ þatei
nimiþ, yah waírþiþ izwis.
25 Yah þan standáiþ
bidyandans, aflētáiþ, yabái
ƕa habáiþ wiþra ƕana, ei
yah atta izwar sa in
himinam aflētái izwis
missadedins izwarōs.

26 Iþ yabái yus ni aflētiþ,
ni þáu atta izwar sa in
himinam aflētiþ izwis
missadēdins izwaros.
27 Yah iddyēdun aftra du
Iaírusaulwmái, yah in alh
ƕarbōndin imma,
atiddyēdun du imma þai
aúhumistans gudyans yah
bokaryos yah sinistans.

20 And in the morning, as
they passed by, they saw the
fig tree dried up from the
roots.
21 And Peter calling to
remembrance saith unto
him, Master, behold, the fig
tree which thou cursedst is
withered away.
22 And Jesus answering
saith unto them, Have faith
in God.
23 For verily I say unto
you, That whosoever shall
say unto this mountain, Be
thou removed, and be thou
cast into the sea; and hall
not doubt in his heart, but
shall believe that those
things which he saith shall
come to pass; he shall have
whatsoever he saith.
24 Therefore I say unto
you, What things soever ye
desire, when ye pray,
believe that ye receive them,
and ye shall have them.
25 And when ye stand
praying, forgive, if ye have
ought against any: that your
Father also which is in
heaven may forgive you
your trespasses.
26 But if ye do not forgive,
neither will your Father
which is in heaven forgive
your trespasses.
27 And they come again to
Jerusalem: and as he was
walking in the temple, there
come to him the chief
priests, and the scribes, and
the elders,

28 Yah qēþun du imma, in
ƕamma waldufnyē þata
tauyis? Yah ƕas þus þata
waldufni atgaf, ei þata
táuyis?
29 Iþ Iesus andhafyands
qaþ du im, fraíhna yah ik
izwis áinis waúrdis yah
andhafyiþ mis, yah qiþa
izwis in ƕamma waldufnyē
þata táuya,
30 dáupeins Iōhannis uzuh
himina was þáu uzuh
mannam? Andhafyiþ mis.
31 Yah þáhtēdun du sis
missō qiþandans, yabai
qiþam, us himina, qiþiþ,
aþþan duƕē ni
galáubidēduþ imma?
32 Ak qiþam, us mannam,
ūhtēdun þō managein. Allái
áuk alakyō habaidēdun
Iōhannēn þatei bi sunyai
prauf ētēs was
33 Yah andhafyandans
qēþun du Iēsua, ni witum.
Yah andhafyands Iēsus qaþ
du im, nih ik izwis qiþa in
ƕamma waldufnyē þata
táuya.

28 And say unto him, By
what authority doest thou
these things? and who gave
thee this authority to do
these things?
29 And Jesus answered
and said unto them, I will
also ask of you one
question, and answer me,
and I will tell you by what
authority I do these things.

30 The baptism of John,
was it from heaven, or of
men? Answer me.
31 And they reasoned with
themselves, saying, If we
shall say, From heaven, he
will say, Why then did ye
not believe him?
32 But if we shall say, of
men, they feared the people:
for all men counted John,
that he was a prophet
indeed.
33 And they answered and
said unto Jesus, We cannot
tell. And Jesus answering
saith unto them, Neither do
I tell you by what authority I
do these things.

CHAPTER 12

12:1 Yah dugann im in
gayukōm qiþan, weinagard
ussatida manna yah bisatida
ina faþōm yah usgrōf dal uf
mēsa yah gatimrida kēlikn
yah anafalh ina
waurstwyam yah afláiþ
alyaþ.

CHAPTER 12

12:1 And he began to speak
unto them by parables. A
certain man planted a
vineyard, and set an hedge
about it, and digged a place
for the winefat, and built a
tower, and let it out to
husbandmen, and went into
a far country.

2 Yah insandida du þáim
waúrstwyam at mēl skalk, ei
at þaim waurstwyam nēmi
akranis þis weinagardis.

3 Iþ eis nimandans ina
usbluggwun yah
insandidēdun láushandyan.

4 Yah aftra insandida du im
anþarana skalk, yah þana
stáinam wairpandans
gaáiwiskōdēdun yah
háubiþwundan brāhtēdun
yah insandidēdun
ganáitidana.
5 Yah aftra insandida
anþarana; yah yáinana
afslōhun yah managans
anþarans, sumans
usbliggwandans, sumanzuh
þan usqimandans.
6 Þanuh naúhþanuh áinana
sunu áigands liubana sis,
insandida yah þana du im
spedistana, qiþands þatei
gaáistand sunu meinana.
7 Iþ yáinái þái waúrstwyans
qēþun du sis missō þatei sa
íst sa arbinumya; hiryiþ,
usqimam imma, yah unsar
waírþiþ þata arbi.
8 Yah undgreipandans ina
usqēmun, yah uswaúrpun
imma ūt us þamma
weinagarda.
9 Ƕa nuh táuyái fráuya þis
weinagardis? Qimib yah
usqisteiþ bans waúrstwyans,
yah gibiþ þana weinagard
anþaráim.

2 And at the season he sent
to the husbandmen a
servant, that he might
receive from the
husbandmen of the fruit of
the vineyard.
3 And they caught him, and
beat him, and sent him
away empty.
4 And again he sent unto
them another servant; and
at him they cast stones, and
wounded him in the head,
and sent him away
shamefully handled.

5 And again he sent
another; and him they
killed, and many
others; beating some, and
killing some.
6 Having yet therefore one
son, his well beloved, he
sent him also last unto
them, saying, They will
reverence my son.
7 But those husbandmen
said among themselves,
This is the heir; come, let us
kill him, and the inheritance
shall be our's.

8 And they took him, and
killed him, and cast him out
of the vineyard.
9 What shall therefore the
lord of the vineyard do? he
will come and destroy the
husbandmen, and will give
the vineyard unto others.

10 Nih þata gamēlidō ussuggwuþ, stains þammei uswaúrpun þái timryans, sah warþ du háubida waíhstins?

11 Fram fráuyin warþ sa, yah ist sildaleiks in áugam unsaráim.

12 Yah sōkidēdun ina undgreipan, yah ōhtēdun þō managein; frōþun auk þatei du im þō gayukōn qaþ. Yah aflētandans ina galiþun.

13 Yah insandidēdun du imma sumái þizē Fareisaiē yah Hērōdianē, ei ina ganuteina waúrda

14 Iþ eis qimandans qēþun du imma, láisari, witum þatei sunyeins is yah ni kara þuk manshun; ni auk saíƕis in andwaírþya mannē, ak bi sunyái wig Gudis láiseis, skuldu ist kaisaragild giban kaisara, þáu niu gibáima ?

15 Iþ Iēsus gasaíƕands izē liutein qaþ du im, ƕa mik fráisiþ? Atbaíriþ mis skatt, ei gasaíƕáu.

16 Iþ eis atbērun, yah qaþ du im, ƕis ist sa manleika yah so uíarmēleins? Iþ eis qēþun du imma; kaisaris.

17 Yah andhafyands Iēsus qaþ du im, usgibiþ þō kaisaris kaisara yah þō Gudis Guþa. Yah sildaleikidēdun ana þamma.

10 And have ye not read this scripture; The stone which the builders rejected is become the head of the corner:

11 This was the Lord's doing, and it is marvellous in our eyes?

12 And they sought to lay hold on him, but feared the people: for they knew that he had spoken the parable against them: and they left him, and went their way.

13 And they send unto him certain of the Pharisees and of the Herodians, to catch him in his words.

14 And when they were come, they say unto him, Master, we know that thou art true, and carest for no man: for thou regardest not the person of men, but teachest the way of God in truth: Is it lawful to give tribute to Caesar, or not?

15 Shall we give, or shall we not give? But he, knowing their hypocrisy, said unto them, Why tempt ye me? bring me a penny,that I may see it.

16 And they brought it. And he saith unto them, Whose is this image and superscription? And they said unto him, Caesar's.

17 And Jesus answering said unto them, Render to Caesar the things that are Caesar's, and to God the things that are God's. And they marvelled at him.

18 Yah atiddyēdun
Saddukaieis du ímma þáiei
qiþand usstass ni wisan, yah
frēhun ina qiþandans,
19 Láisari, Mōsēs gamēlida
unsis þatei yabái ƕis brōþar
gadáuþnái, yah bileiþái
qēnái, yah barnē ni
bileiþái, ei nimái brōþar is
þō qēn is, yah ussatyái
barna brōþr seinamma.

20 Sibun brōþrahans
wēsun; yah sa frumista nam
qēn, yah gaswiltands ni
biláiþ fráiwa.
21 Yah anþar nam þō; yah
gadáuþnōda, yah ni sa biláiþ
fráiwa.

22 Yah nēmun þō
samaleikō þái sibun, yah ni
biliþun fráiwa. Spedumista
alláizē gaswalt yah so qēns.
23 In þizái usstassái, þan
usstandand, ƕaryamma izē
waírþiþ qēns? Þái auk sibun
áihtēdun þō du qēnái.

24 Yah andhafyands Iēsus
qaþ du im; niu duþē aírzyái
siyuþ, ni kunnandans mela
nih maht Gudis?
25 Allis þan usstandand us
dáuþáim, ni liugand ni
liuganda, ak sind swē
aggilyus þái in himinam.

18 Then come unto him the
Sadducees, which say there
is no resurrection; and they
asked him, saying,
19 Master, Moses wrote
unto us, If a man's brother
die, and leave his wife
behind him, and leave no
children, that his brother
should take his wife, and
raise up seed unto his
brother.
20 Now there were seven
brethren: and the first took
a wife, and dying left no
seed.
21 And the second took
her, and died, neither left he
any seed: and the third
likewise.
22 And the seven had her,
and left no seed: last of all
the woman died also.

23 In the resurrection
therefore, when they shall
rise, whose wife shall she be
of them? for the seven had
her to wife.
24 And Jesus answering
said unto them, Do ye not
therefore err, because ye
know not the scriptures,
neither the power of God?
25 For when they shall rise
from the dead, they neither
marry, nor are given in
marriage; but are as the
angels which are in heaven.

26 Aþþan bi dáubans, þatei
urreisand, niu
gakunnáidēduþ ana bōkōm
Mōsēzis ana
aíƕatundyái, ƕáiwa imma
qaþ guþ qiþands. ik im Guþ
Abrahamis yah Guþ Isakis
yah Iakōbis?

27 Nist Guþ dáuþáizē, ak
qiwáizē. Aþþan yus filu
aírzyái siyuþ.

28 Yah duatgaggands áins
þizē bōkaryē, gaháusyands
ins samana sōkyandans,
gasaíƕands þatei waíla im
andhōf, frah ina, ƕarya ist
alláizō anabusnē frumista?
29 Iþ Iēsus andhōf imma;
þatei frumista alláizō
anabusns, háusei Israel,
fráuya Guþ unsar fráuya
áins ist.
30 Yah friyōs fráuyan Guþ
þeinana us allamma haírtin
þeinamma yah us allái
sáiwalái þeinái yah us allái
gahugdái þeinái yah us allái
mahtái þeinái. Sō frumista
anabusns.
31 Yah anþara galeika þizái,
friyōs nēƕundyan þeinana
swē þuk silban. Máizei þáim
anþara anabusns nist.
32 Yah qaþ du imma sa
bōkareis: waíla, Láisari, bí
sunyái qast þatei áins ist,
yah nist anþar alya imma;

26 And as touching the
dead, that they rise: have ye
not read in the book of
Moses, how in the bush God
spake unto him, saying, I
am the God of Abraham,
and the God of Isaac, and
the God of Jacob?
27 He is not the God of the
dead, but the God of the
living: ye therefore do
greatly err.
28 And one of the scribes
came, and having heard
them reasoning together,
and perceiving that he had
answered them well, asked
him, Which is the first
commandment of all?
29 And Jesus answered
him, The first of all the
commandments is, Hear, O
Israel; The Lord our God is
one Lord:
30 And thou shalt love the
Lord thy God with all thy
heart, and with all thy soul,
and with all thy mind, and
with all thy strength: this is
the first commandment.
31 And the second is like,
namely this, Thou shalt love
thy neighbour as thyself.
There is none other
commandment greater than
these.
32 And the scribe said unto
him, Well, Master, thou hast
said the truth: for there is
one God; and there is none
other but he:

33 yah þata du friyōn ina
us allamma haírtin yah us
allamma fraþya yah us allái
sáiwalái yah us allái mahtái,
yah þata dufriyōn
nēƕundyan swē sik silban
managizō ist alláim þáim
alabrunstim yah sáudim.
34 Yah Iēsus gasaíƕands
ina þatei frōdaba
andhōf, qaþ du imma, ni
faírra is þiudangardyái
Gudis. Yah áinshun
þanaseiþs ni gadaúrsta ina
fraíhnan.
35 Yah andhafyands Iēsus
qaþ láisyans in alh; ƕáiwa
qiþand þái y þatei Xristus
sunus ist Daweidis?
36 Silba áuk Daweid qaþ in
Ahmin Weihamma, qiþiþ
fráuya du fráuyin
meinamma, sit af taíhswōn
meinái, untē ik galagya
fiyands þeinans fōtubaúrd
fōtiwē eináizē.
37 Silba rafhtis Daweid
qiþiþ ina fráuyan, yah
ƕaþrō imma sunus ist? Yah
alla so managei háusidēdun
imma gabaúryaba.
38 Yah qaþ du im in
láiseinái seinái, saíƕiþ faúra
bō*karyam* ...

CHAPTER 13

13:16 ... wastya seina.

33 And to love him with all
the heart, and with all the
understanding, and with all
the soul, and with all the
strength, and to love his
neighbour as himself, is
more than all whole burnt
offerings and sacrifices.
34 And when Jesus saw
that he answered discreetly,
he said unto him, Thou art
not far from the kingdom of
God. And no man after that
durst ask him any question.
35 And Jesus answered
and said, while he taught in
the temples, How say the
scribes that Christ is the son
of David?
36 For David himself said
by the Holy Ghost, The
LORD said to my Lord, Sit
thou on my right hand, till I
make thine enemies thy
footstool.

37 David therefore himself
calleth him Lord; and
whence is he then his son?
And the common people
heard him gladly.
38 And he said unto them
in his doctrine, Beware of
the scribes, which love to go
in long clothing, and love
salutations in the
marketplaces,

CHAPTER 13

13:16 And let him that is in
the field not turn back again
for to take up his garment.

17 Aþþan wái þáim qiþuhaftōm yah daddyandeim in yáináim dagam.

17 But woe to them that are with child, and to them that give suck in those days!

18 Aþþan bidyáiþ ei ni waírþái sa þlaúhs izwar wintráu.

18 And pray ye that your flight be not in the winter.

19 Waírþanđ áuk þái dagos yáinái aglo swaleika, swē ni was swaleika fram anastōdeinái gaskaftáis þōei gaskōp Guþ, und hita, yah ni waírþiþ.

19 For in those days shall be affliction, such as was not from the beginning of the creation which God created unto this time, neither shall be.

20 Yah ni fráuya gamaúrgidēdi þans dagans, ni þáuh ganēsi áinhun leikē, akei in þizē gawalidanē þanzei gawalida, gamaúrgida þans dagans.
21 Yah þan yabái ƕas izwis qiþái, sái, her Xristus, aíþþáu sái, yáinar, ni galáubyáiþ;
22 untē urreisand galiugaxristyus yah galiugapraúfēteis, yah giband táiknins yah faúratanya du afaírzyan, yabái mahteig siyái, yah þans gawalidans.
23 Iþ yus saíƕiþ, sái, faúragatáih izwis allata

20 And except that the Lord had shortened those days, no flesh should be saved: but for the elect's sake, whom he hath chosen, he hath shortened the days.
21 And then if any man shall say to you, Lo, here is Christ; or,lo, he is there; believe him not:
22 For false Christs and false prophets shall rise, and shall shew signs and wonders, to seduce, if it were possible, even the elect.

23 But take ye heed: behold, I have foretold you all things.

24 Akei in yáinans dagans afar þō aglōn yáina sauil riqizeiþ yah mēna ni gibiþ liuhaþ sein.

24 But in those days, after that tribulation, the sun shall be darkened, and the moon shall not give her light,

25 Yah staírnōns himinis
waírþand driusandeins yah
mahteis þōs in himinam
gawagyanda.
26 Yah þan gasaíƕand
sunu mans qimandan in
milhmam miþ mahtái
managái yah wuiþáu.
27 Yah þan insandeiþ
aggiluns seinans yah galisib
þans gawali-dans seinans af
fidwōr
windam fram andyam
aírþōs und andi himinis.

25 And the stars of heaven
shall fall, and the powers
that are in heaven shall be
shaken.
26 And then shall they see
the Son of man coming in
the clouds with great power
and glory.
27 And then shall he send
his angels, and shall gather
together his elect from the
four winds, from the
uttermost part of the earth
to the uttermost part of
heaven.

28 Aþþan af smakkabagma
ganimib þō gayukōn. Þan
þis yuþan asts þlaqus
waírþiþ yah uskeinand
láubōs, kunnuþ þatei neƕa
ist asans.
29 Swah yah yus, þan
gasaƕriþ þata waírþan,
kunneiþ þatei nēƕa siyuþ a*t*
...

28 Now learn a parable of
the fig tree; When her
branch is yet tender, and
putteth forth leaves, ye
know that summer is near:
29 So ye in like manner,
when ye shall see these
things come to pass, know
that it is nigh, even at the
doors.

CHAPTER 14

14:4 ...*fraqis*teins þis
balsanis warþ?

5 Maht wēsi áuk þata
balsan frabugyan in
managizō þáu þriya hunda
skattē, yah giban unlēdáim.
Yah andstaúrráidēdun þō.

6 Iþ Iēsus qaþ, lētiþ þō;
duƕē izái usþriutiþ? Þannu
gōþ waúrstw waúrhta bi
mis.

CHAPTER 14

14:4 And there were some
that had indignation within
themselves, and said, Why
was this waste of the
ointment made?
5 For it might have been
sold for more than three
hundred pence, and have
been given to the poor. And
they murmured against her.
6 And Jesus said, Let her
alone; why trouble ye her?
she hath wrought a good
work on me.

7 Sinteinō áuk þans
unlēdans habáiþ miþ izwis,
yah þan wileiþ, maguþ im
waíla táuyan; iþ mik ni
sinteinō habáiþ.
8 Þatei habáida so
gatawida, faúrsnáu salbōn
mein leik du usfilha.

9 Amen, qiþa izwis;
þisƕaruh þei mēryada so
aíwaggēlyō and alia
manasēþ, yah þatei
gatawida so rōdyada du
gamundái izōs.

10 Yah ludas Iskariōteis,
áins þizē twalibē, galáiþ du
þáim gudyam, ei galēwidēdi
ina im.
11 Iþ eis gaháusyandans
faginōdēdun yah
gahaíháitun imma faíhu
giban, yah sōkida ƕáiwa
gatilaba ina galēwidēdi.

12 Yah þamma frumistin
daga azymē, þan paska
salidēdun, qēþun du imma
þái sipōnyōs is: ƕar wileis ei
galeiþandans manwyáima,
ei matyáis paska?

13 Yah insandida twans
sipōnyē seináizē qaþuh du
im, gaggats in þō baúrg, yah
gamōteiþ igqis manna kas
watins baírands, gaggats
afar þamma,

7 For ye have the poor with
you always, and whensoever
ye will ye may do them
good: but me ye have not
always.
8 She hath done what she
could: she is come
aforehand to anoint my
body to the burying.
9 Verily I say unto you,
Wheresoever this gospel
shall be preached
throughout the whole world,
this also that she hat done
shall be spoken of for a
memorial of her.
10 And Judas Iscariot, one
of the twelve, went unto the
chief priests, to betray him
unto them.
11 And when they heard it,
they were glad, and
promised to give him
money. And he sought how
he might conveniently
betray him.
12 And the first day of
unleavened bread, when
they killed the passover, his
disciples said unto him,
Where wilt thou that we go
and prepare that thou
mayest eat the passover?
13 And he sendeth forth
two of his disciples, and
saith unto them, Go ye into
the city, and there shall
meet you a man bearing a
pitcher of water: follow him.

14 yah þadei inngaleiþái, qiþáits þamma heiwafráuyin þatei láisareis qiþiþ, ƕar sind saliþwōs þarei paska miþ sipōnyam meináim matyáu?

15 Yah sa izwis táikneiþ kēlikn mikilata, gastrawiþ, manwyata; yah yáinar manwyáiþ unsis.
16 Yah usiddyēdun þái sipōn*yōs*...

41 ... sái, galēwyada sunus mans in handuns frawaúrhtáíze.

42 Urreisiþ, gaggam! Sái, sa lēwyands mik atnēƕida.
43 Yah sunsáiw naúhbanuh at imma rōdyandin qam ludas, sums bizē twalibē, yah miþ imma managei miþ haírum yah triwam fram þáim aúhumistam gudyam yah bōkaryam yah sinistam.

44 Atuh-þan-gaf *ina* sa lēwyands im bandwōn qiþands, þammei kukyáu, sa ist, greipiþ þana yah tiuhiþ arniba.
45 Yah qimands sunsáiw, atgaggands du imma qaþ, Rabbei, Rabbei, yah kukida imma.

14 And wheresoever he shall go in, say ye to the goodman of the house, The Master saith, Where is the guest chamber, where I shall eat the passover with my disciples?
15 And he will shew you a large upper room furnished and prepared: there make ready for us.
16 And his disciples went forth, and came into the city, and found as he had said unto them: and they made ready the passover.
41 And he cometh the third time, and saith unto them, Sleep on now, and take your rest: it is enough, the hour is come;... behold, the Son of man is betrayed into the hands of sinners.
42 Rise up, let us go; lo, he that betrayeth me is at hand.
43 And immediately, while he yet spake, cometh Judas, one of the twelve, and with him a great multitude with swords and staves, from the chief priests and the scribes and the elders.

44 And he that betrayed him had given them a token, saying, Whomsoever I shall kiss, that same is he; take him, and lead him away safely.
45 And as soon as he was come, he goeth straightaway to him, and saith, Master, master; and kissed him.

46 Iþ eis uslagidēdun
handuns ana ina yah
undgripun ina.
47 Iþ áins sums þizē
atstandandanē imma
uslūkands haíru slōh skalk
aúhumistins gudyins yah
afslōh irnma áusō þata
taíhswō.
48 Yah andhafyands Iēsus
qaþ du im, swē du
wáidēdyin urrunnuþ miþ
haírum yah
triwam greipan mik.
49 Daga ƕammēh was at
izwis in alh láisyands yah ni
gripuþ mik; ak ei
usfullnōdēdeina bōkōs.

50 Yah aflētandans ina
gaþlaúhun allái.
51 Yah áins sums
yuggaláuþs láistida afar
imma biwáibiþs leina ana
naqadana, yah gripun is þái
yuggaláudeis.
52 Iþ is bileiþands þamma
leina naqaþs gaþláuh faúra
im.
53 Yah gataúhun Iēsu du
aúhumistin gudyin, yah
garunnun miþ imma
aúhumistans gudyans allái
yah þái sinistans yah
bōkaryōs.

54 Yah Paítrus faírraþrō
láistida afar imma, untē
qam in garda bis
aúhumistins gudyins; yah
was sitands miþ andbahtam
yah warmyands sik at
liuhada.

46 And they laid their
hands on him, and took
him.
47 And one of them that
stood by drew a sword, and
smote a servant of the high
priest, and cut off his ear

48 And Jesus answered
and said unto them, Are ye
come out, as against a thief,
with swords and with staves
to take me?

49 I was daily with you in
the temple teaching, and ye
took me not: but the
scriptures must be fulfilled.

50 And they all forsook
him, and fled.
51 And there followed him
a certain young man, having
a linen cloth cast about his
naked body; and the young
men laid hold on him:
52 And he left the linen
cloth, and fled from them
naked.
53 And they led Jesus away
to the high priest: and with
him were assembled all the
chief priests and the elders
and the scribes.

54 And Peter followed him
afar off, even into the palace
of the high priest: and he sat
with the servants, and
warmed himself at the fire.

55 Iþ þái aúhumistans
gudyans yah alla so
gafaúrds sōkidēdun ana Iēsu
weitwōdiþa du afdáuþyan
ina yah ni bigētun.
56 Managái áuk galiug
weitwōdidēdun ana ina, yah
samaleikōs þōs weitwōdiþōs
ni wēsun.
57 Yah sumái
usstandandans galiug
weitwōdidēdun ana ina
qiþandans,
58 þatei weis
gaháusidēdum qiþandan ina
þatei ik gataíra alh þō
handuwaúrhtōn, yah bi
þrins dagans anþara
unhanduwaurhta gatimrya.

59 Yah ni swa samaleika
was weitwōdiba izē.
60 Yah usstandands sa
aúhumista gudya in
midyáim frah Iēsu qiþands,
niu andhafyis waíhí, ƕa þái
ana þuk weitwōdyand?

61 Iþ is þaháida yah waíht
ni andhōf. Aftra sa
aúhumista gudya frah ina
yah qaþ du Imma;
þu is Xristus sa sunus þis
þiuþeigins?

55 And the chief priests
and all the council sought
for witness against Jesus to
put him to death; and found
none.
56 For many bare false
witness against him, but
their witness agreed not
together.
57 And there arose certain,
and bare false witness
against him, saying,

58 We heard him say, I will
destroy this temple that is
made with hands, and
within three days I will
build another made without
hands.

59 But neither so did their
witness agree together.
60 And the high priest
stood up in the midst, and
asked Jesus,saying,
Answerest thou nothing?
what is it which these
witness against thee?
61 But he held his peace,
and answered nothing.
Again the high priest asked
him, and said unto him, Art
thou the Christ, the Son of
the Blessed?

62 Iþ is qaþuh, ik im; yah
gasaíƕiþ þana sunu mans af
taíhswōn sitandan mahtáis,
yah qimandan miþ
milhmam himinis.

62 And Jesus said, I am:
and ye shall see the Son of
man sitting on the right
hand of power, and coming
in the clouds of heaven.

63 Iþ sa aúhumista gudya
disskreitands wastyōs
seinōs qaþ, ƕa þanamáis
þaurbum weis weitwōdē?
64 Háusidēduþ þō waya-
mērein is; ƕa izwis
þugkeiþ? Þaruh eis allái
gadōmidēdun ina skulan
wisan dáuþáu.
65 Yah dugunnun sumái
speiwan ana wlit is yah
hulyan andwaírþi is yah
káupatyan ina, yah qēþun
du imma, praúfētei yah
andbahtōs lōfam slōhun ina.
66 Yah wisandin Paítráu in
rōhsnái dalaþa atiddya áina
þiuyō þis aúhumistins
gudyins,
67 yah gasafƕandei Paítru
warmyandan sik,
insaíƕandei du imma qaþ,
yah þu miþ Iēsua þamma
Nazōreináu wast.
68 Iþ is afaíáik qiþands, ni
wait, ni kann ƕa þu qiþis.
Yah galáiþ faúr gard, yah
hana wōpida.

63 Then the high priest
rent his clothes, and saith,
What need we any further
witnesses?
64 Ye have heard the
blasphemy: what think ye?
And they all condemned
him to be guilty of death.

65 And some began to spit
on him, and to cover his
face, and to buffet him, and
to say unto him, Prophesy:
and the servants did strike
him with the palms of their
hands.
66 And as Peter was
beneath in the palace, there
cometh one of the maids of
the high priest:
67 And when she saw Peter
warming himself, she
looked upon him,and said,
And thou also wast with
Jesus of Nazareth.
68 But he denied, saying, I
know not, neither
understand I what thou
sayest. And he went out into
the porch; and the cock
crew.

69 Yah þiwi gasaíƕandei
ina aftra dugann qiþan þáim
faúrastandandam, þatei sa
þizei ist.

69 And a maid saw him
again, and began to say to
them that stood by, This is
one of them.

70 Iþ is aftra láugnida. Yah
afar leitil aftra þái
atstandandans qēþun du
Paítráu, bi sunyái, þizei is;
yah auk Galeilaius is yah
razda þeina galeika ist.
71 Iþ is dugann afáikan yah
swaran þatei ni kann þana
mannan þanei qiþiþ.

72 Yah anþaramma sinþa
hana wōpida. Yah gamunda
Paítrus þata waúrd, swē qaþ
imma Iēsus, þatei faúrþizē
hana hrukyái twáim sinþam,
inwidis mik þrim sinbam.
Yah dugann greitan.

CHAPTER 15

15:1 Yah sunsáiw in
maúrgin garūni táuyandans
þái aúhumistans gudyans
miþ þáim sinistam yah
bōkaryam, yah alla so
gafaúrds gabindandans Iēsu
brāhtēdun ina at Peilātáu.

2 Yah frah ina Peilātus, þu
is þiudans Iudaiē? Iþ is
andhaf-yands qaþ du imma,
þu qiþis.

3 Yah wrōhidēdun ina þái
aúhumistans gudyans filu.

4 Iþ Peilātus aftra frah ina
qibands, niu andhafyis ni
waíht? Sáí, ƕan filu ana þuk
weítwōdyand.

70 And he denied it again.
And a little after, they that
stood by said again to Peter,
Surely thou art one of them:
for thou art a Galilaean, and
thy speech agreeth thereto.

71 But he began to curse
and to swear, saying, I know
not this man of whom ye
speak.
72 And the second time the
cock crew. And Peter called
to mind the word that Jesus
said unto him, Before the
cock crow twice, thou shalt
deny me thrice. And when
he thought thereon, he
wept.

CHAPTER 15

15:1 And straightway in the
morning the chief priests
held a consultation with the
elders and scribes and the
whole council, and bound
Jesus, and carried him
away, and delivered him to
Pilate.
2 And Pilate asked him, Art
thou the King of the Jews?
And he answering said unto
them, Thou sayest it.
3 And the chief priests
accused him of many things:
but he answered nothing.
4 And Pilate asked him
again, saying, Answerest
thou nothing? behold how
many things they witness
against thee.

5 īþ lēsus þanamáis *waiht*
ni andhōf, swaswē
sildaleikida Peilātus.
6 Iþ and dulþ ƕaryōh
fralaílōt im áinana bandyan
þanei bēdun.

7 Wasuh þan sa háitana
Barabbas miþ þáim miþ
imma drōbyandam
gabundans, þáiei in
aúhyōdáu maúrþr
gatawidēdun.
8 Yah usgaggandei alia
managei dugunnun bidyan,
swaswē sinteinō tawida im.

9 Iþ Peilātus andhōf im
qiþands, wileidu fraleitan
izwis þana þiudan ludaiē?

10 Wissa áuk þatei in
neiþis atgēbun ina þái
aúhumistans gudyans.
11 Iþ þái aúhumistans
gudyans inwagidēdun þō
managein ei máis Barabban
fralaílōti im.
12 Iþ Peilātus aftra
andhafyands qaþ du im, ƕa
nu wileiþ ei táuyáu þammei
qiþiþ þiudan ludaiē?

13 Iþ eis aftra hrōpidēdu,
ushramei ina.
14 Iþ Peilātus qab du im, ƕa
allis ubilis gatawida? Iþ eis
máis hrōpidēdun; ushramei
ina.

5 But Jesus yet answered
nothing; so that Pilate
marvelled.
6 Now at that feast he
released unto them one
prisoner, whomsoever they
desired.
7 And there was one named
Barabbas, which lay bound
with them that had made
insurrection with him, who
had committed murder in
the insurrection.
8 And the multitude crying
aloud began to desire him to
do as he had ever done unto
them.
9 But Pilate answered
them, saying, Will ye that I
release unto you the King of
the Jews?
10 For he knew that the
chief priests had delivered
him for envy.
11 But the chief priests
moved the people, that he
should rather release
Barabbas unto them.
12 And Pilate answered and
said again unto them, What
will ye then that I shall do
unto him whom ye call the
King of the Jews?
13 And they cried out
again, Crucify him.
14 Then Pilate said unto
them, Why, what evil hath
he done? And they cried out
the more exceedingly,
Crucify him.

15 Iþ Peilātus wílyands
þizái managein
fullafahyan, fralaílōt im
þana Barabban, iþ Iēsu atgaf
usbliggwands, ei ushramiþs
wēsi
16 Iþ gadradhteis gataúhun
ina innana gardis, þatei íst
praítōriaún, yah
gahaíháítun alla hansa,
17 yah gawasidēdun ina
paúrpurái, yah atlagidēdun
ana ina þaúrneina wipya
uswindandans,
18 yah dugunnun gōlyan
ina, hails, þiudan Iudaiē!
19 Yah slōhun is háubiþ
ráusa, yah bispiwun ina, yah
lagyandans kniwa inwitun
ina.

20 Yah biþē bilaíláikun ina
andwasidēdun ina þizái
paúrpurái, yah gawasidēdun
ina wastyōm swēsáim, yah
ustaúhun ina ei
ushramidēdeina ina.
21 Yah undgripun sumana
mannē, Seimōna Kwreinaiu,
qimandan af akra, attan
Alaíksandráus yah Rufáus,
ei nēmi galgan is.

22 Yah attaúhun ina ana
Gaúlgaúþa staþ þatei ist
gaskeiriþ ƕaírneins staþs.

23 Yah gēbun imma
drigkan wein miþ smwrna,
iþ is ni nam.

15 And so Pilate, willing to
content the people, released
Barabbas unto them, and
delivered Jesus, when he
had scourged him, to be
crucified.
16 And the soldiers led him
away into the hall, called
Praetorium; and they call
together the whole band.
17 And they clothed him
with purple, and platted a
crown of thorns, and put it
about his head,
18 And began to salute
him, Hail, King of the Jews!
19 And they smote him on
the head with a reed, and
did spit upon him, and
bowing their knees
worshipped him.
20 And when they had
mocked him, they took off
the purple from him, and
put his own clothes on him,
and led him out to crucify
him.
21 And they compel one
Simon a Cyrenian, who
passed by, coming out of the
country, the father of
Alexander and Rufus, to
bear his cross.
22 And they bring him
unto the place Golgotha,
which is, being interpreted,
The place of a skull.
23 And they gave him to
drink wine mingled with
myrrh: but he received it
not.

24 Yah ushramyandans ina
disdáilyand wastyōs is
waírpandans hláuta ana
þōs, ƕaryizuh ƕa nēmi.
25 Wasuh þan ƕeila
þridyō, yah ushramidēdun
ina.

26 Yah was ufarmēli
faírinōs is ufarmēliþ "Sa
þiudans Iudaiē".

27 Yah miþ imma
ushramidēdun twans
wáidēdyans, áinana af
taíhswōn yah áinana af
hleidumein is.
28 Yah usfullnōda þata
gamēlidō þata qiþanō; "Yah
miþ unsibyáim rahniþs
was".
29 Yah þái faúrgaggandans
wayamēridēdun ina,
wiþōndans háubida seina
yah qiþandans, Ō sa
gataírands þō alh yah bi
þrins dagans gatimryands
þō,
30 nasei þuk silban yah
atsteig af bamma galgin.
31 Samaleikō yah þái
aúhumistans gudyans
biláikandans ina miþ sis
missō miþ þáim bōkaryam
qeþun, anþarans ganasida;
iþ sik silban ni mag
ganasyan.
32 Sa Xristus, sa þiudans
Israēlis, atsteigadáu nu af
þamma galgin, ei
gasaíƕáima yah
galáubyáima. Yah þái miþ
ushramidans imma
idweitidēdun imma.

24 And when they had
crucified him, they parted
his garments, casting lots
upon them, what every man
should take.
25 And it was the third
hour, and they crucified
him.
26 And the superscription
of his accusation was
written over, *THE KING OF
THE JEWS.*
27 And with him they
crucify two thieves; the one
on his right hand, and the
other on his left.
28 And the scripture was
fulfilled, which saith, And
he was numbered with the
transgressors.
29 And they that passed by
railed on him, wagging their
heads, and saying, Ah, thou
that destroyest the temple,
and buildest it in three days,

30 Save thyself, and come
down from the cross.
31 Likewise also the chief
priests mocking said among
themselves with the scribes,
He saved others; himself he
cannot save.

32 Let Christ the King of
Israel descend now from the
cross, that we may see and
believe. And they that were
crucified with him reviled
him.

33 Yah biþē warþ ƕeila
saíhstō, riqis warþ ana allái
aírþái und ƕeila niundōn.
34 Yah niundōn ƕeilái
wōpida lēsus stibnái mikilái
qiþands, aílōe aílōē, lima
sibakþanei, þatei ist
gaskeiriþ, Guþ meins, Guþ
meins, duƕē mis biláist?

35 Yah sumái þizē
atstandandanē
gaháusyandans qēþun, sái,
Hēlian wōpeiþ.
36 Þragyands þan áins yah
gafullyands swam akeitis,
galag- yands ana ráus,
dragkida ina qiþands, lēt, ei
saíƕam qimáiu Hēlias
athafyan ina.

37 Iþ lēsus aftra lētands
stibna mikila uzōn.

38 Yah faúrahāh alhs
disskritnōda in twa iupaþrō
und dalaþ.
39 Gasaíƕands þan sa
hundafaþs sa atstandands in
andwaírþya is þatei swa
hrōpyands uzōn, qaþ, bi
sunyái, sa manna sa sunus
was Gudis.
40 Wēsunuþ-þan qinōns
faírraþrō saíƕandeins, in
þáimei was Marya so
Magdalēnē yah Marya
lakōbís þis minnizins yah
lōsēzis áiþei yah Salome.

33 And when the sixth
hour was come, there was
darkness over the whole
land until the ninth hour.
34 And at the ninth hour
Jesus cried with a loud
voice, saying, Eloi, Eloi,
lama sabachthani? which is,
being interpreted, My God,
my God, why hast thou
forsaken me?
35 And some of them that
stood by, when they heard
it, said, Behold, he calleth
Elias.
36 And one ran and filled a
sponge full of vinegar, and
put it on a reed, and gave
him to drink, saying, Let
alone; let us see whether
Elias will come to take him
down.
37 And Jesus cried with a
loud voice, and gave up the
ghost.
38 And the veil of the
temple was rent in twain
from the top to the bottom.
39 And when the
centurion, which stood over
against him, saw that he so
cried out, and gave up the
ghost, he said, Truly this
man was the Son of God.
40 There were also women
looking on afar off: among
whom was Mary
Magdalene, and Mary the
mother of James the less
and of Joses, and Salome;

41 Yah þan was in Galeilaia, yah láistidēdun ina yah andbahtidēdun imma, yah anþarōs managōs þōzei miþ iddyēdun imma in Iaírusalēm.

42 Yah yuþan at andanahtya waúrþanamma, untē was Paraskaíwē, saei ist fruma sabbatō.

43 Qimands Iōsēf af Areímaþaias, gaguds ragineis, saei was *yah* silba beidands þiudangardyōs gudis, ananaþyands galáiþ inn du Peilātáu yah baþ þis leikis Iēsuis.

44 Iþ Peilātus sildaleikida ei is yuþan gaswalt; yah atháitands þana hundafaþ frah ina yuþan gadáuþnōdēdi.

45 Yah finþands at þamma hundafada fragaf þata leik Iōsēfa.

46 Yah usbugyands lein yah usnimands ita biwand þamma leina yah galagida ita in hláiwa þatei was gadraban us stáina, yah atwalwida stáin du daúra þis hláiwis.

47 Iþ Marya sō Magdalēnē yah Marya Iōsēzis sēƕun ƕar galagibs wēsi.

41 (Who also, when he was in Galilee, followed him, and ministered unto him;) and many other women which came up with him unto Jerusalem.

42 And now when the evening was come, because it was the preparation, that is, the day before the sabbath,

43 Joseph of Arimathaea, an honourable counsellor, which also waited for the kingdom of God, came, and went in boldly unto Pilate, and craved the body of Jesus.

44 And Pilate marvelled if he were already dead: and calling unto him the centurion, he asked him whether he had been any while dead.

45 And when he knew it of the centurion, he gave the body to Joseph.

46 And he bought fine linen, and took him down, and wrapped him in the linen, and laid him in a sepulchre which was hewn out of a rock, and rolled a stone unto the door of the sepulchre.

47 And Mary Magdalene and Mary the mother of Joses beheld where he was laid.

CHAPTER 16

16:1 Yah inwisandins
sabbatē dagis Marya sō
Magdalēnē yah Marya sō
Iakōbis yah Salōmē
usbaúhtēdun arōmata, ei
atgaggandeins
gasalbōdēdeina ina.
2 Yah filu áir þis dagis
afarsabbatē atiddyēdun du
þamma hláiwa at
urrinnandin sunnin.

3 Yah qēþun du sis missō,
ƕas afwalwyái unsis þana
stáin af daúrōm þis hláiwis?

4 Yah insaíƕandeins
gáumidēdun þammei
afwalwiþs ist sa stáins, was
áuk mikils abraba.
5 Yah atgaggandeins in
þata hláiw gasēƕun
yuggaláuþ sitandan in
taíhswái biwáibidana
wastyái ƕeitái, yah
usgeisnōdēdun.
6 Þaruh qaþ du im, ni
faúrhteiþ izwis, Iēsu sōkeiþ
Nazōraiu þana ushramidan;
nist hēr, urráis, sái þana
staþ þarei galagidēdun ina.
7 Akei gaggiþ qiþiduh du
sipōnyam is yah du Paítráu
þatei faúrbigaggiþ izwis in
Galeilaian; þaruh ina
gasaíƕiþ, swaswē qaþ izwis.

CHAPTER 16

16:1 And when the sabbath
was past, Mary Magdalene,
and Mary the mother of
James, and Salome, had
bought sweet spices, that
they might come and anoint
him.
2 And very early in the
morning the first day of the
week, they came unto the
sepulchre at the rising of the
sun.
3 And they said among
themselves, Who shall roll
us away the stone from the
door of the sepulchre?
4 And when they looked,
they saw that the stone was
rolled away: for it was very
great.
5 And entering into the
sepulchre, they saw a young
man sitting on the right
side, clothed in a long white
garment; and they were
affrighted.
6 And he saith unto them,
Be not affrighted: Ye seek
Jesus of Nazareth, which
was crucified: he is risen; he
is not here: behold the place
where they laid him.
7 But go your way, tell his
disciples and Peter that he
goeth before you into
Galilee: there shall ye see
him, as he said unto you.

8 Yah usgaggandeins af
þamma hláiwa gaþlaúhun,
dizuh-þan-sat iyōs reirō yah
usfilmei, yah ni qēþun
mannhun waíht, ōhtēdun
sis áuk.
9 Usstandands þan in
maúrgin frumin sabbatō
atáugida *sik*frumist Maryin
þizái Magdalēnē, af þizáiei
uswarp síbun unhulþōns.

10 Sōh gaggandei gatáih
þáim miþ imma wisandam,
qáinōndam yah grētandam.

11 Yah eis háusyandans
þatei libáiþ yah gasaíƕans
warþ fram izái, ni
galáubidēdun.
12 Afaruh þan þata **...**

8 And they went out
quickly, and fled from the
sepulchre; for they trembled
and were amazed: neither
said they any thing to any
man; for they were afraid.
9 Now when Jesus was
risen early the first day of
the week, he appeared first
to Mary Magdalene, out of
whom he had cast seven
devils.
10 And she went and told
them that had been with
him, as they mourned and
wept.
11 And they, when they
heard that he was alive, and
had been seen of her,
believed not.
12 After that he appeared
in another form unto two of
them, as they walked, and
went into the country...

BACKGROUND

Gothic is an extinct East Germanic language, related to Old English and Danish. Presumably mutually intelligible dialects of East Germanic languages were once spoken by peoples such as Ostrogoths, Visigoths, Gepids, Vandals, Burgundians, and others.

During the fourth century AD, Goths lived in what is now Romania, Ukraine, and Bulgaria, on the northeast border of the Roman Empire. During this century the Goths were converted to Christianity, largely through the efforts of Bishop Wulfila. Bishop Wulfila, c. 311 –383, known also as Ulfilas or Urphilas, was a 4th century Gothic evangelist considered to be the apostle to the Gothic nations, who is credited with translating the Bible into Gothic. (Bennett, 1980, p. 22-23.) Wulfila, (little-wolf,) was initially a church lector in Gothia, a role which required considerable Biblical study.

This was a fractious era in early Christianity which saw multiple Christian denominations that each considered themselves the orthodox, or correct faith, while holding all others to be heretics.

Furthermore, churches in the Roman East commonly used the vernacular language as a liturgical language thus, Wulfila's services were conducted in the Gothic language. However, Orthodox churches in the Roman West only used Latin, even in areas where Latin was not common. This became a source of conflict once Goths moved into the Latin West. Gothic most likely continued as a liturgical language for the Gothic Church after its adherents began to speak Latin.

Wulfila's converts were to become the first European church founded outside of the Roman Empire, and thus a little-known but important part of early Christian history.

Gothic Christians experienced fierce persecution under pagan Gothic Kings who considered Christianity to be a pernicious infiltration of Roman influence, (Heather, 1998, p. 73,74, 304.) The Christian Goths Wereka and Batwin and others were martyred by royal decree two years before St. Sabbas the Goth was martyred in c. 372 C.E.. Three years later, twenty-six Gothic Christians in the Crimea were burned alive. These martyred Christians were to be canonized by the church. (Wolfram, 1988, p. 81-83, 96.)

According to the church historian Philostorgius, Wulfila was sent by the Goths during the reign of Constantine I as an ambassador to the Roman Empire. Wulfila was consecrated as bishop of Gothia by the bishop of Constantinople, Eusebius of Nicomedia, about 341 C.E. Emperor Constantius II, a son of Constantine the Great, apparently described Wulfila as the contemporary Moses; Bishop Wulfila was also compared to the prophet Elijah in his lifetime, (Wolfram, 1988, p. 76.)

St. Wulfila invented the Gothic alphabet for the purpose of translating the Bible into the Gothic language. Reputedly, the Books of I-II Kings were not translated, as Goths were warlike enough. Bishop Wulfila is known to have written Christian sermons in Latin, Greek, and Gothic, and was deeply respected by Goths for centuries to come for his devotion. Sozomenus the historian states that later Goths believed their spiritual father Wulfila could do no wrong. (Bennett, 1980, p. 23.)

This early Biblical translation by Wulfila became only the third effort to render the Bible into another language, after Syriac and Latin. This was also the first Biblical translation of a language from beyond the northern, barbarian, borders of the Roman Empire. Bishop Wulfila's Gothic language Bible was to be widely received and read for centuries to come. Gothic-speaking churches sprouted up even in Constantinople and Ravenna. Gothic legionnaires surely brought Wulfila's Bible with them to Britain and to Persia. It is reasonable to infer that other East Germanic speakers besides Goths used Bishop Wulfila's Bible. The love for this translation is evident today in that most notable of Gothic manuscripts, the magnificent, purple and silver Codex Argenteus, of Ostrogothic origin. Wulfila's Bible is a valuable monument of early Christianity.

In the later 300s, Goths fell under assault by nomads from Asia called the Huns, (Maenchen-Helfen,1973, p. 18-30.) In turn Goths fled into Roman territory in 376 C.E... Romans and allied Goths fought the Huns and their allied Goths under King Attila. There were so many East Germanic speakers under the Huns that Gothic became the de facto lingua fraca of the Hunnic Empire.

The Visigoths followed Alaric to conquer Rome on August 24, 410 C.E. (Jones, Dan. 2021, p. 51.) St. Augustine wrote *City of God* in response to the fall of Rome to the Visigoths, (Dixon, 1976, p. 17.) The Vandals took North Africa, Anglo-Saxons invaded Britain. The Franks occupied modern France. The Gepids, an East Germanic group, quietly occupied what is now roughly the area of Romania, Serbia, and Hungary. (Dixon,

1976, p. 9-15.) Burgundians, also East Germanic speakers, settled in western Switzerland and northern France; their fall to the Romans and their Hun allies in 436 C.E. inspired the literary classic, *The Nibelungenlied.*

Romans in vain attempts to stave off destruction slaughtered massive numbers of non-combatant Goths. (Dixon, 1976, p. 11.) This was the beginning of the Age of Migrations, a violent and chaotic time in Europe's history encompassing the fall of the West Roman Empire, which was carved up into multiple kingdoms and disappeared. (Dixon, 1976, p. 21.)

Gothic speakers migrated across Europe. East Germanic speakers were some of the prime movers and shakers in the Early Medieval world. In any timeline of European history, Goths and other East Germanic speakers are that thin wedge between the Roman era and Medieval times.

The Visigoths established a kingdom in southern France and Iberia with their capital in Toledo. The Ostrogoths forged a vibrant Classical kingdom in Italy. Gothic Christianity existed side by side with other sects in these areas for centuries before upheavals brought the dominance of the Catholic Church. The East Roman Empire ended the Ostrogothic Kingdom only by mass deportations of Ostrogoths as slaves throughout the eastern Mediterranean. A Frankish invasion removed Visigothic rule from southern France.

For a certain length of time, the Mediterranean was ringed by Gothic or East Germanic speakers, in an arc from Crimea, west through the Balkans, south to Constantinople, north through the Pannonian plains, west through Italy, to southern France, down through Iberia, across to Roman Africa, (contemporary Tunisia, Algeria,) and possibly further east, to Egypt. One Gothic text was discovered in Egypt, the Codex Gissensis, a Gothic-Latin bilingual copy of Luke, indicating there was at least one East Germanic speaker in Egypt. (The Latin text, found in the Greek-speaking East Roman Empire, may indicate someone from the Ostrogothic diaspora.) Linguists moreover point to possible etymological evidence that Goths ran Christian missions to the pagan peoples of what is now Germany and Austria, (Green, 2008, 308-324.)

During the very late Roman Empire, Goths joined the Roman Senate. (Heather, 1998, p. 256.) A Roman named Cyprianus, who worked in the Ostrogothic cabinet under King Theodoric, attained to the highest ranks of Patricius, Magister Officiorum, court treasurer, and Senator, and had his sons taught the Gothic language, (Heather, 1998, p. 257.) Cyprianus apparently considered a working knowledge of Gothic to be essential education. We don't know how many other Romans followed suit; for someone to have attained Cyprianus' illustrious ranks was to be an influencer of the highest order. As King Theodoric is quoted as saying, "A poor Roman plays the Goth; a rich Goth, a Roman," (Heather, 1998, p. 257.) Perhaps only in Ostrogothic Italy, but Gothic in spirit was developing into a Classical language alongside Greek and Latin.

Sadly, all Gothic texts were deliberately burned in the Visigothic Kingdom in Iberia in 589 C.E. following doctrinal conflicts. The Visigoths under King Reccared I converted to Catholicism following the Third Council of Toledo. The victors successfully burned all Gothic manuscripts in Iberia as heretical. The Visigothic church was a strong Christian leader until it's cataclysmic destruction after the Islamic invasion of 711, still, the Visigothic Mozarabic Rite, as it became known, has survived. Gothic texts were probably destroyed also at the fall of the Ostrogoths and of the Vandals.

The ninth century monk Walafrid Strabo wrote that Gothic was still being used as a liturgical language in Costantsa, Romania, in his time; the Gothic Bible seems to have fallen from use after this, (Bennett, 1980, p. 18-19.) The Gotica Parasina, a 9th century manuscript from northern France, documents that someone then still was familiar with Gothic. Graffiti from a basilica at Mangup, Crimea proves that the Gothic language and Wulfila's alphabet were still in use there in the 9th century; Crimean Gothic managed to survive the Middle Ages until the 16th century in Crimea.

A mere fraction of Wulfila's translation currently survives; all known texts are degraded. Some texts are palimpsests, meaning a parchment in which a Gothic text was erased, in order to re-use the parchment page for another text, but which leaves yet the Gothic writing impression.

Notable Christians in the Gothic world include Bishops Theophilus of Gothia and Cadmus of Bosporus from the Crimea, who were both signatories at the First Council of Nicaea in 325 C.E.. Bishop Wulfila. Bishop Selenas. Bishop Arius, (is his name "*Arjaus" in Gothic, from *Arjausdags, the postulated origin for the Bavarian name for Tuesday? (Mine. Green, 2008, 244.) St. Augustine. St. Isidore of Seville, the current saint of the internet. Cassiodorus. Jordanes. King Sisebut. Dracontius, Saint Eulalia. Bishop Masona. The philosopher Boethius. Leovigild. King Theodoric. Queen

Amalasuntha. St. Sabbas the Goth. Gaiseric. King Roderic. King Ardo. Ennodius, and many more.

Based on canonization practices of the times, miracle workers, the devout, clerics, royalty who aided the church, or the martyred could all become saints. Bishop Wulfila assuredly was venerated as a saint by Gothic Christians, (Wolfram, 1988, p. 77.) We don't have the surviving records to know empirically who was canonized in the Gothic church. Many of the above-mentioned people may have been considered saints by Goths.

THE GOTHIC ALPHABET

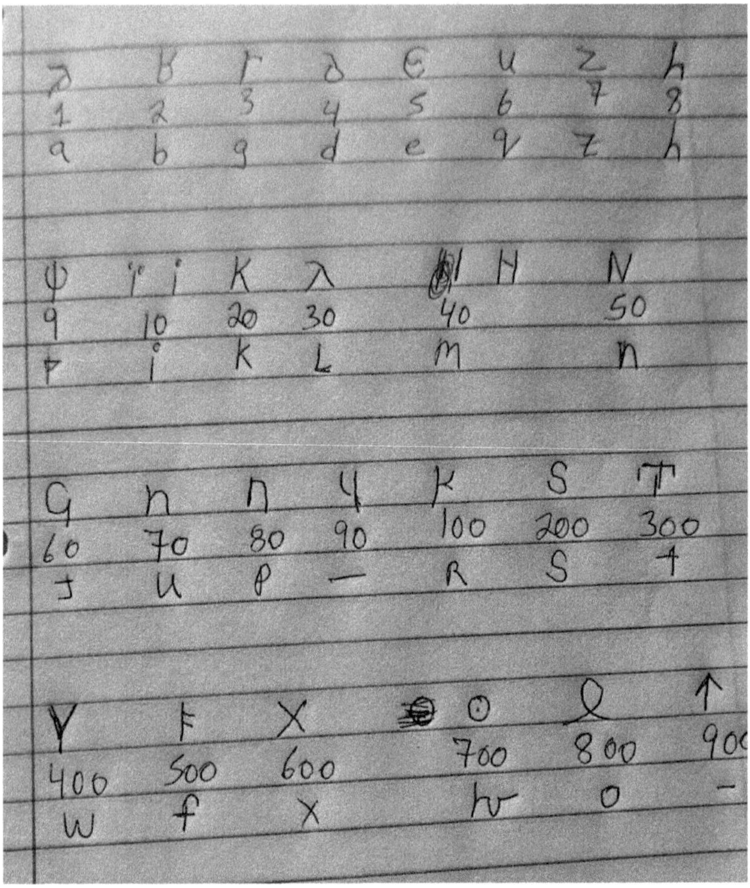

A hand drawing of the Gothic alphabet, after Wright. There are multiple web sites that depict the alphabet in better detail. Wulfila's alphabet is increasingly preferred over the Roman for Gothic.

The Gothic alphabet was invented by Bishop Wulfila, apostle to the Goths; Wright said: "The Gothic monuments, as handed down to us, are written in a peculiar alphabet which, according to the Greek ecclesiastical historians Philostorgios and Sokrates, was invented by Ulfilas, (Wulfila,) But Wimmer' and others have clearly shown that Ulfilas simply took the Greek uncial alphabet as the basis for his, and that in cases where this was insufficient for his purpose he had recourse to the Latin and runic alphabets. The alphabetic sequence of the letters can be determined with certainty from the numerical values, which agree as nearly as possible with those of the Greek." (Joseph Wright, *Grammar of the Gothic language*. 1910. P. 4.)

BIBLIOGRAPHY

A Gothic alphabet font: https://robertpfeffer.net/schriftarten/englisch/nachgeladener_rahmen.html?skeirs_runen.html

A Gothic alphabet picture. https://commons.wikimedia.org/wiki/File:Gothic_alphabet.png

Bachrach, Bernard S.. *A History of the Alans in the West: From Their First Appearance in the Sources of Classical Antiquity through the Early Middle Ages*. University of Minnesota Press. 1973.

Barnes, Timothy *"The Consecration of Ulfila"*. The Journal of Theological Studies. 41 (2). Oxford University Press: 541–545. JSTOR 23965598. 1990.

Bennett, William H.. *An Introduction to the Gothic Language*. Modern Language Assn. of America, 1980.

Bennett, William H.. *The Gothic Commentary on the Gospel of John: Skeireins Aiwaggeljons Thairh Iohannen*. Modern Language Assn. of America, 1960.

Bible. King James Version. Public Domain, 1611.

Bosworth, Joseph Rev. D. D. F.R.S. F.S. A.. *The Gothic and Anglo-Saxon Gospels in Parallel Columns, with the Versions of Wycliffe and Tyndale*. 3rd edition. London; Reeves and Turner. 1888.

Burns, Thomas. *A History of the Ostrogoths*. Indiana University Press, 1991.

Bury, J.B.. *The Invasion of Europe by the Barbarians*. Norton Library. 1967.

Collins, Roger. *Visigothic Spain 409 – 711*. Wiley-Blackwell, 2004

Dixon, Philip. *Barbarian Europe*. E.P. Dutton and Co. Inc. 1976.

Friedrichsen, G.W.S.. *The Gothic Version of the Epistles*. Oxford University Press, 1939.

Friedrichsen, G.W.S.. *The Gothic Version of the Gospels*. Oxford University Press, 1926.

Falluomini, Carla. *The Gothic Version of the Gospels and Pauline Epistles: Cultural Background, Transmission and Character*. Berlin: de Gruyter. ISBN 978-3-11-033469-2. 2015.

Green, D.H. *Language and History in the Early Germanic World.* Cambridge University Press; ISBN-13: 978-0521794237. 2008.

Heather, Peter. *The Goths.* Blackwell Publishers Ltd., 1998.

Heather, Peter; Matthews, John. *The Goths in the Fourth Century.* Liverpool University Press, 1991.

Heyne's Gothic Dictionary:
http://www.ling.upenn.edu/~kurisuto/germanic/goth_heyne_about.html

St. Isidore of Seville. *History of the Goths, Vandals, and Suevi. Independently published. 2023.*

Jones, Arthur, Wiseman, Robin. *The Goths, Children of the Storm. iUniverse, Inc., 2009.*

Jones, Dan. *Powers and Thrones.* Viking Press. 2021.

Jordanes. *The Origin and Deeds of the Goths.* Dodo Press, 1908.

Koebler's Gothic etymological dictionary:
http://www.koeblergerhard.de/gotwbhin.html

Lambdin, Thomas O.. *An Introduction to the Gothic Language.* Ancient Language Resources, 2006.

Lauritzen, Frederick . *"The Gothic Psalter between Crimea and Bologna".* Revue des Études Tardo-Antiques.: 109–120. 2019.

https://www.lexilogos.com/english/gothic_dictionary.htm Has Bishop Wulfila's alphabet.

Maenchen-Helfen, Otto. *The World of the Huns.* University of California Press. 1973.

Marcelinus, Ammianus. *The Later Roman Empire (A.D. 354-378.)* Penguin Books. 1986.

Miller, D. Gary *The Oxford Gothic Grammar.* Oxford University Press. ISBN 9780198813590. 2019.

Musset, Lucien. *The Germanic Invasions.* The Pennsylvania State University Press. 1975.

Nordgren, Ingemar. *The Well Spring of the Goths.* iUniverse. 2004.

Pennick, Nigel. *The Inner Mysteries of the Goths.* Capall Bann Publishing. 1995.

Project Wulfila: http://www.wulfila.be/

Rubin, Zeev *"The Conversion of the Visigoths to Christianity".* Museum Helveticum [de]. *38 (1).* Schwabe Verlag*: 34–54.* JSTOR 24815706. 1981.

Sivan, Hagith. *"Ulfila's Own Conversion".* The Harvard Theological Review. *89 (4).* Cambridge, Massachusetts*:* Cambridge University Press*: 373–386.* JSTOR 1509923. 1996.

Snaedal, Magnús. *A Concordance to Biblical Gothic Vol. I and II*. Institute of Linguistics, University of Iceland, University of Iceland Press, 1998.

Snaedal, Magnús. *Gotic Contact with Latin, Gotica Parisina and Wulfila's Alphabet* https://www.academia.edu/13032710/Gotic_Contact_with_Latin_Gotica_Parisina_and_Wulfilas_Alphabet#:~:text=Abstract,influence%20of%20the%20Latin%20alphabet. 2015.

Streitberg, Wilhelm. *Die Gotische Bibel*. Carl Winter, Heidelberg Universitaetsverlag. 1919.

Thompson, E.A..*The Goths in Spain*. Oxford University Press, 1969.

Thompson, E.A.. *The Visigoths in the Time of Ulfila*. Gerald Duckworth & Co. Ltd., 2008.

Thorsson Edred. *The Mysteries of the Goths*. Lodestar Books 2011.

Todd Malcolm. Everyday life of the Barbarians: Goths, Franks and Vandals. Everyday Life, 1972.

Vasiliev, Alexander Alexandrovich. *The Goths in the Crimea*. The Medieval Academy of America, 1936.

Wolfram, Herwig. *History of the Goths*. University of California Press, 1988.

Wright, Joseph. *Grammar of the Gothic Language*. Oxford, 1910.

ABOUT THE EDITOR

Gregory Scaff was raised in Clearwater, Florida. He hails from a family of educators and clergy. Gregory attended the Universität Wien and holds a degree in Anthropology from U.S.F.

Gregory has studied Theology and has ministered as a deacon and as a cleric on a Church Council.

Gregory is a polymath who has taught classes & workshops in art, Anthropology, poetry, Early Medieval History, medieval art, and in Gothic history.

Gregory is a conlanger, a poet, an artist, and a philosopher.

Gregory served as a consultant for the film *Conlanging, the Art of Crafting Tongues*, by Britton Watkins.

Gregory frequents Mid-Atlantic poetry readings. His poetry & his Dada poetry have been published in *Obelisk Magazine, Circle Works, The Valley Literary Magazine, New Reality Magazine,* and in *Aequinox IV, Carpazine,* and more. Gregory also self-publishes mini-chapbooks and zines of his poetry.

Gregory's paintings can be seen in Mid-Atlantic shows and galleries.

Gregory lives with his brilliant daughter and his Muse of a wife.

SEE ALSO

Scaff, Gregory. *Succubus Arts*. ISBN 978-0-9970129-0-3. A Fantasy erotica poetry book. Cambridge, MD: Succubus Media. 2023.

Ed. by Scaff, Gregory. *The Visigothic Mark*. ISBN 978-0-9970129-3-4. A Gothic & English Interlinear Edition. 2026.

Scaff, Gregory, *Whoraxia, Lilac & Leonine*. ISBN: 978-0-9970129-4-1 . Poetry. . Cambridge, MD: Succubus Media. 2025.

POETRY BITES

Scaff, Gregory. *The Abandoned and The Undead.* Annapolis, MD: Succubus Media. 2012. Print. OOP.

Scaff, Gregory. *Breast Clamps.* Annapolis, MD: Succubus Media. 2019. Print. Poetry Bite. OOP.

Scaff, Gregory. *Dramatic Theme Swells.* Annapolis, MD: Succubus Media. 2020. Print. Poetry Bite. OOP.

Scaff, Gregory. *Furball.* Burlington, VT: Succubus Media, 2004. Print. A poetry zine written completely in runes. OOP.

Scaff, Gregory, *Kettle Memento Mori.* Annapolis, MD: Succubus Media. 2019. Print. Poetry Bite. OOP.

Scaff, Gregory. *Nymph.* Annapolis, MD: Succubus Media. 2019. Print. Poetry Bite. OOP.

Scaff, Gregory. *Odin's Legislations.* Clearwater, Fl: Succubus Media. 1980. Print. OOP.

Scaff, Gregory. *Platinum Blondage.* Annapolis, MD: Succubus Media. 2014. Print. OOP.

Scaff, Gregory. *Poems, Prayers, and Curses.* Burlington, VT: Succubus Media. 2000. Print. Poetry Bite. OOP.

Scaff, Gregory. *Towards a More Respectful Language: The Need for a Neutral Third Person Pronoun.* Burlington, VT: Succubus Media. 2000. Print. OOP.

Scaff, Gregory. *A Taazhpuur Grammar & Lexicon.* Annapolis, MD: Succubus Media. 2013. Print. OOP.

COLLECTIONS

Gregory Scaff's work has been collected in these esteemed institutions:
The Carter/Johnson Leather Library and Collection.
The Department of Constructed Languages Collection of the Austrian National Library.
The Leather Archives & Museum.
The Museum of Menstruation.
The Museum of Sex.

Gregory's paintings are in private collections worldwide.

REVIEWS

Gregory's paintings were in an art show called *From the Storm*, reviewed in *Newsweek*, December 13, 1993.

Gregory's s work is referenced in the book *Women, Art, and Technology* by Judy Malloy, MIT Press. 2003. page 301.

UPCOMING

SuccubusMedia is pleased to announce that Gregory Scaff will publish *A Taazhpuur-English Dictionary* as soon as next year.

SuccubusMedia is pleased to announce that Gregory Scaff will publish a collection of Dada poetry, including a much-awaited manifesto.

SUCCUBUSMEDIA

SuccubusMedia is a small press based in Maryland, USA, that primarily publishes poetry, Gotica, and exotica through online POD. Thank you for reading this book, you rock.

20SVCCVBVSMEΔIA26

www.ingramcontent.com/pod-product-compliance
Lightning Source LLC
LaVergne TN
LVHW011047110826
845149LV00015B/3386